AS SEEN ON
OWN Network's *Super Soul Sunday*

THE SOUL'S COACH

7 PATHS

to Healing Your Relationship

Rochelle L. Cook MA., ChT.

For permission requests, write to the publisher, addressed "Attention: Permissions Coordinator," at the address below.
Bloom Factor Press
4115 Glencoe Avenue, Suite 105
Marina del Rey, CA 90292
www.bloomfactor.com

Ordering Information:
Quantity sales. Special expanded wholesale availability is available on quantity purchases by corporations, associations, and others. For details, contact the publisher CreateSpace >>> www.createspace.com/pub/l/ createspacedirect.do or order it through one of the regular wholesalers, e.g., Ingram.

ISBN-10: 0-9891931-2-8
ISBN-13: 978-0-9891931-2-2

Library of Congress In-Publication Data
Cook MA., ChT. Rochelle L.
The Soul's Coach – 7 Paths to Healing Your Relationship
1. Spirituality 2. Psychology 3 Self Help

Project, cover and book design directed by Michael Glock Ph.D.
Typesetting by Ramesh Kumar
Interior typeset in Sabon (body) & Oswald (Chapter)
Front/back cover art work by © Gregg Chadwick Used by permission:
May 10 2016 www.greggchadwick.com/

Printed in the United States of America
BFP 14 13 12 11 10 9 8   7 6 5 4   3 2 1

Disclaimer

This book is not intended as a substitute for the medical advice of physicians or licensed mental health professionals. The reader should regularly consult a physician in matters relating to his/her health, mental health and particularly with respect to any symptoms that may require diagnosis or medical attention.

Some names and identifying details have been changed to protect the privacy of individuals.

For my daughter,
May the words in this book guide you down your path!
You are the greatest gift I will ever receive
Thank you for loving me
It is my privilege to call you my child

To all of my clients
Thank you for trusting me
Thank you for your stories
Thank you for your wisdom
and
Thank you for your love

Acclaim for Rochelle L. Cook MA., ChT.

THE SOUL'S COACH - 7 PATHS TO HEALING YOUR RELATIONSHIP

I was struggling with so many issues that seemed to just pile on and I was overwhelmed. A friend suggested that I call Rochelle. I'd always traveled the traditional therapy road; so quite frankly, I didn't know what to expect.

What I found was someone incredibly intuitive, gentle, and laser-focused on what my issues were, and more importantly, what my options for solution might be. Rochelle takes time, she listens, and her feedback is nothing short of extraordinary. Meeting her was a gift, enormously helpful, and she left me with tools to better navigate my "stuff." I cannot recommend Rochelle enough. She's the real deal.

T.D. New York, NY

Wow! What can I say other than Rochelle is one of the most amazingly authentic people on the planet. Even when walking through some of my darkest moments I never felt judgment or discomfort when I am doing work with her. I have seen a lot of people for therapy and other inner work-they all pale in comparison to the work that Rochelle naturally does. I HIGHLY recommend Rochelle if you have blocks or if you suffer from anything mentally, spiritually or physically, as she is a true miracle worker! I will always utilize her services as she makes me feel beyond good during and after our sessions!!

Amy F. Seattle, WA

Rochelle is an inspiring and intelligent person. She has helped me so quickly with so many deep rooted issues that I feel like I have been stuck with for so long. I cannot thank her enough for helping me start a new journey. Her technique works, and it is a wonderful to be in her company.

I have never tried hypnotherapy before, but I am so grateful to have found Rochelle because I have realized that is she gives so much more. She is an incredible spiritual guide, filled with light and love.

India W. Venice, California, USA

I strongly recommend Rochelle as a therapist. I went in to see Rochelle based on a good recommendation by a friend because I was dealing with difficult family relationships stemming from the recent passing of a parent. I gained so much from her incredibly accurate and helpful analysis, and she provides a number of powerful visualization and spiritual exercises that helped me gain a better and healthier perception of others and myself. I feel as though a great weight has been lifted off my shoulders and I look forward to continued work with such a great professional.

Tim C. Venice, California, USA

Rochelle gets five stars because she is DEDICATED TO HELPING OTHERS & she has the SKILL SET TO DO IT. Her experience, training, intuitive nature & compassion helped me connect with my past and guided me through a TRANSFORMATIONAL PROCESS that gave me understanding and freedom. I HIGHLY RECOM-MEND you to meet with Rochelle and experience this for yourself. Thank you Rochelle for all you have given me so far.

Maxine W. Los Angeles, California, USA

Rochelle is the real deal! She is extremely articulate, smart, honest and warm. She gained my trust almost instantaneously, she is incredible. Ask for what you want and you shall receive with this miracle worker. She has changed my life and I've only had 4 sessions.

Annie P. Manhattan, NY

Transformational is an apt description of the experience derived from Rochelle's expertise. With her intuitive, intelligent and enthusiastic approach to hypnosis, she brought an astonishing amount of clarity and peace in our sessions. She is a warm, spiritual and sensitive person and a brilliant communicator. I immediately felt comfortable with her and confident in her abilities. The process is fascinating, enjoyable and very effective. I highly recommend Rochelle to anyone grappling with the many issues she is dedicated to healing.

Michele P. Beverly Hills, California, USA

Contents

FORWARD

On a very beautiful early spring morning thirty five years ago, two young people graduated from the same university. They were very much alike. They had been told early on in life to "follow their bliss." Both had been great students, both were gregarious and well adjusted to the world, and both – as young graduates are – were filled with hope, ambition and dreams for the future. Recently I met these two people. They were still very much alike, both were in fulfilling relationships, one was married one was not. One was healthier than the other; one had put on more weight. And both, it turned out, were working in similar fields. But there was a difference. One of them was an unhappy manager on a sixth career path and the other was a successful leader and CEO of a Fortune 500 firm.

What made the difference?

Imagine that one of the people described above is you. Have you ever wondered, as I have, what makes this kind of difference in people's lives? It isn't always native intelligence, or education or creative talent or commitment or dedication. It isn't that one person focused on success and the other didn't. The difference exists in what each person knows and has experienced, and how they have worked their flaws and failures into knowledge and success.

This book is full of wise and practical processes that you can use to work your flaws and failures into knowledge and success. In its own personal and unique way, the book generously offers a set of actionable tools that you can practice while reading. It's full of tested lessons written by a wounded soul who has transformed herself into a remarkable healer. Rochelle's gift as a Soul's Coach and clinical hypnotherapist is to professionally and intuitively analyze the wounds of her clients and mirror this insight back. Even the mere action of reading the book will bring about a healing experience in the reader. While reading each page, your life may very well change and shift. These pages are the crucible that tenderly marinates your perceived negative experiences and transforms them into a sacred life. You will begin by identifying your imperfections, complexes and flaws, thereby uncovering your 'self' as you've known it all your life. As you progress through the *7-Paths*, your small 'self,' with a lowercase s, will inadvertently reveal your real 'Self' – with a capital S. This book is an initiation into wise and valuable teachings from Spiritual and Depth psychology and Jungian psychology. Frankly, it is about finding balance and a harmonious state of mind that unify the consciousness and unconsciousness in a person.

Wise knowledge is power

Reading the book, I was thinking of a sculptor's way of working. The sculptor views a block of raw marble and focuses on its flaws and imperfections, just as you, dear reader, will discover that the way through is the way down – through your anxiety, distress, pain and suffering. As the sculptor carves out the marble's imperfections, allowing the beauty of the sculpture to emerge, so chipping at your imperfections will allow the beauty of who you are meant to be, to emerge.

If you are reading this Forward you may have synchronistically been drawn towards wise knowledge. If you have reached an impasse of one sort or another, perhaps a wounding of your personality has, or is occurring, perhaps love is missing, or something is not functioning well in your work, career or vocation, *The Soul's Coach - 7 Paths to Healing Your Relationship* is your medicine. This book is an innovative guide that illuminates the deep and hidden longing of your soul. Page by page, *path* by *path*, you will experience renewed strength, confidence, competence, and a healthy, loving and generous creative vision for yourself and others.

This Process Appears Nowhere Else.

Back to those two people I mentioned in the beginning of this Forward: They graduated from the same university together and together got started in the world. So what made their lives different?

Wise Knowledge, useful knowledge, and its application in the world.

I cannot promise you that such wise knowledge or success will be instantly yours if you start reading *The Soul's Coach - 7 Paths to Healing Your Relationship*. But I can guarantee that you will find this book fascinating, creative and always an investment in your success.

Sincerely yours,
Michael Glock Ph.D.

ACKNOWLEDGMENTS

firstly want to acknowledge my mother. Without your permission, strength, honesty and courage, I would have not been able to write this book. Your life story, love, compassion and wisdom have guided me down my own healing path. You are my lighthouse, my bright, shinning star.

Jet, thank you, if you had not called 911, I would not be here to write this book. You saved my life. Watching you watch me has forced me to become the mother I am today. You are my child and my teacher, my treasure, remember that!

Thank you to my husband Michael! Our conversations about depth psychology, spirituality, and the lessons life has served us both are an endless inspiration. I value the stories we share and the light they shed on our relationship. Our own story has become a highlight in my life – a cause for celebration.

To my dad, thank you for taking me under your wing and sheltering me from the cold. Your teaching, "Be tough and keep going," is forever etched deep within my soul and comes to my aid whenever I need it. Karen, thank you for teaching me to fight. Giving up was never a question.

My best friend Paula, and Soul Sister Mary, your daily phone calls and home and hospital visits reminded me to keep the faith and that "I will be okay." I know that you were checking up on me, your eagle eyes could see my tears, and your compassion protected me from the sea of darkness. Thank you for loaning me your strength.

Yann Peron, even though our marriage may be over, our friendship has bloomed. You and your family have been instrumental in my life. The Peron teachings are anchors in my life. Thank you for allowing me to become part of your family.

To my good friends and teachers, you know who you are – your support and encouragement have been overwhelming. Sometimes we all need a little help. Difficult times are hard to face alone, and you never let me remain alone. For all the times you have gone out of your way to help me – I thank you from the bottom of my heart.

Jonas Elrod, thank you for highlighting my work on abandonment in your TV series. You turned on the light on my life's purpose. Relationships and abandonment are important to fix. Thank you for your trust and respect.

With great affection I thank my creative consultant and editor, Elana Golden. Your talent and perseverance have helped me to record my life's work. As we both agree, helping others is a gift.

To my mentor Dr. Ronald Hulnick your teachings enlightned my journey, lightened my soul and have inspired me to assist others on their way home. Dr. Mari Beech thank you for teaching me how to trust spirit, your words of wisdom have been etched into my life forever. The two of you have made me into what I have become.

Last but not least, thank you Spirit! Your lessons have not always been easy to learn, but I now understand their purpose. Thank you for holding my hand during very difficult times, especially in the last year, as I have been recovering from my surgery. Your lessons are invaluable! Thank you for standing by my side, guiding and inspiring me as I help others. You have blessed me, and I have found my life's calling. Thank you.

But let there be spaces in your togetherness

and let the winds of the heavens dance between you.

Love one another but make not a bond of love,

let it rather be a moving sea between the shores of your souls.

Kahlil Gibran

INTRODUCTION

You Can Transform Your Life

"I Am Not What Happened to Me, I Am What I Choose to Become."

– *C.G. Jung*

D o you ever wonder why you keep choosing the wrong partner or attract the wrong person into your life? Do you have trouble getting over a breakup? Do you experience commitment issues? Are you afraid that someone you love will leave you? Would you like to improve the relationship you are now in? What mind-set or behavior is getting in your way of finding your life-long partner?

If you experience problems in your relationship, or around relationships in general, it is worth taking a look at your beliefs and behaviors. No experience should be minimized. What matters most is how you perceive your experience. Everything we do is in context of relationships, with the relationship to one's self being the most important one. We live in an interconnected world. Our wellbeing depends on our ability to connect to others and to ourselves.

The Soul's Coach – 7 Paths to Healing your Relationship will help you uncover your belief systems and how they affect your life and your relationships. Spiritual Psychology, Hypnotherapy, and other transformational methods I have developed based on my formal studies and personal experience will show you that predominantly *your life is the outcome of your thoughts; change your thinking and your life will change.* This is my philosophy. Your world is made up of perceptions which create your "here and now" reality. If your "here and now" is not to your liking, you have the power to change it by choosing new ways of thinking. Your outer reality is a reflection of your inner reality; whatever is going on "out there" is your mirror that holds the key to your healing. Any relationship is the perfect mirror to look into. When a relationship is blossoming, smile when you look in the mirror; it is your own blossom the mirror is reflecting back to you. When a relationship is problematic or fails all together, look in the mirror; it is your unhealed issues the mirror is reflecting. In resolving these issues and healing the pain of the past you will begin to love and accept yourself as you are, and this in turn will bring into your life the relationship you so desire and deserve.

Learning and practicing the tools discussed in this book will produce long-lasting, effective results. You will see clearly how your subconscious mind controls your life and you will change your subconscious at this deep level, updating irrational negative beliefs into healthy convictions. You will learn to identify your "story" and the behaviors that were formed by your childhood experiences and you will break the pattern – the "story" – and write a new story for your life, one that will support you in living in peace and harmony with yourself and in your relationships.

In the heart of the book I demonstrate the seven paths to healing relationships: Denial, Settling, Playing Out, Acceptance, Intention, Spirituality and The New Story. Each path is infused with the wisdom of Spiritual Psychology, Hypnotherapy and other powerful healing principals. Each path is a stage – a gate – into the inner workings of your life – your subconscious mind that got programmed in your childhood and governs your existence to this day. Just like when tending to a garden you must uproot the dry weeds to enjoy the beautiful flowers, so to gain emotional wellbeing you must uproot your negative thoughts and false beliefs to enjoy a beautiful life. This book will show you how making your subconscious conscious is the way to heal and live the life of your dreams.

Here is the basic question we will return to as we examine your life through the "lens" of each of the seven paths. We will ask it again and again: <u>what was the false lesson you learned as a child that is still playing out in your relationships today?</u>

Perhaps it as simple as, "My father worked and my mother stayed home with the kids. This is the way it is supposed to be." Now this man is married with kids and the wife wants to go back to school and build a career for herself. Unable to see that life could be different from what he had learned in childhood, and with neither wife nor husband having the skills to communicate their needs to each other calmly and logically, the husband screams at his wife, "This is how it should be! You must stay home with the kids and forget about a degree and a career." And so will a present-day conflict, dominated by a false lesson learned in childhood, snowball into physical and verbal abuse, total break in communication, and even divorce.

<u>http://www.yourtango.com/lifestyle</u> *polled 100 mental health professionals and found that communication problems was cited as the most common factor that leads to divorce (65 percent), followed by couples' inability to resolve conflict (43 percent).*

Often children of divorced parents end up themselves divorced or unable to have a healthy relationship. But divorce is only one example. Any trauma or suffering or conflict experienced in childhood is imprinted in our subconscious mind and plays out until we learn to heal and restore those injured parts in ourselves. It is difficult, even impossible, to be in a relationship if our life is run by our past. It is possible to relearn and adopt a new perception of reality that will lead us down a peaceful path.

While this book focuses on relationships, our past is played out in the present time in all areas of our lives: career, vocation, physical and mental health, creative expression, family and community matters. The processes in *The Soul's Coach – 7 Paths to Healing your Relationship* can be applied in all instances where a broken relationship needs mending.

My life story has led me to understand the trauma of abandonment. I was the child left in the dark. Through my own struggles I have learned how to navigate the stormy seas of life. I am more adept now at finding my way out of difficulties. My personal journey and education have prepared me to help those who suffer heal; my deepest wish is to inspire my clients to experience the pleasure of a long lasting relationship.

Why Are Relationships so Hard Sometimes?

Let me be clear. I condemn child abuse and any form of violence at any age. No one "deserves" to suffer. However, spiritually speaking, we all come into this world with a curriculum to face. For some, life is a happy garden full of yellow daffodils – all dreams come true, so easily, so gracefully – for others we wonder why there is so much suffering and tragedy involved. For those who believe in past lives, the belief, or assumption, is that a soul comes into this world with a purpose. This purpose will face obstacles. In the struggle to overcome the obstacles the soul will learn the lessons that will advance it on the ladder of spiritual evolution. Any difficultly or crisis we face is an opportunity to find meaning behind it, heal and grow. The soul of the child chooses its body, its parents, and the life circumstances that will be the best "school" on its evolutionary journey toward wholeness.

One of the ways in which this "school" operates is through projection. What we don't own and admit to in ourselves, we will be presented with in the outer world – and we will hate it! Say your lesson is honesty. You think obsessively about what a liar such and such a person is, and every time you meet this person you feel uncomfortable and your stomach becomes terribly upset because he/ or she is lying again. This is your mirror – your projection – and it's telling you that it's time to look at the lies you yourself are telling. You will see that when you "come clean" about your own lying, you will no longer be disturbed by the person you have previously perceived as such an awful liar. Soon you will no longer attract liars into your life since you have learned and mastered your lesson about honesty. You will no longer need this mirror, this projection.

Being in relationship is the best "school" for personal change and healing as the partners face the "mirror" on a daily basis. Two people come together because they have a mutual spiritual lesson to learn. Relationships tend to magnify all that we are and believe in – in other words, they "push our buttons" – and as such they are potent ground for transformation. But the first step to healing your relationship is healing yourself.

Travelling through the seven paths outlined in this book – Denial, Settling, Playing Out, Acceptance, Intention, Spirituality and The New Story – you will determine where in the process you are, and you will start from there and move in any direction and at any speed your healing is calling you to. One step at a time, you will look at what disturbs your life and you will recall your past to identify the source of your disturbance. You will be astonished to discover how you unconsciously repeat the same pattern over and over even if it is destroying your life. Realizing your responsibility in keeping your pain and suffering alive, you will be able to change your perceptions, let go of the past, and be reborn into the new and exciting you.

I know what I know because through the years of pointing fingers, "he did this, she did that," "I'm not good enough, I'm not worthy," and all the therapists and pills and sorrows that had been my daily bread for so long, the one thing that changed my life was changing my perception.

If you picked up this book I suspect that whether you faced severe trauma or just simply want to be in a healthy relationship, you are ready to take the next step. I applaud you for having the courage to find your way. This book is your ally on the journey to rediscover and live your best you.

Take good care of yourself,
Loving you,
Rochelle

Part 1

CHAPTER ONE

MY STORY

A Childhood That Shaped a Life

My parents divorced when I was five years old and we were still living in Phoenix, Arizona, where I had been born. My father fought for custody, won, and raised me. But I yearned to be with my mother. In nursery school, when all the children played, I would stand by the window waiting for the red signal-light to flash so the cars would stop and I could imagine my mother in her car waving and calling out to me, "I'm around the corner, coming to get you."

After the divorce I moved with my father to California and my mother stayed in Phoenix. I spent holidays and summer vacations with her, and those were wonderful, but on the airplane back home I would cry next to the window all the way to California. Back home, with my dad, stepmother and stepsister, I would keep my fingernail polish on my fingers until it peeled off because it reminded me of my mother. I would cry hysterically on my bedroom floor for hours, feeling so alone.

My mother was a Playboy Bunny and worked as a cocktail waitress in the Playboy Club in Phoenix, Arizona. She was petite with long blond hair and childlike hazel eyes, and wore very short mini skirts, tasseled swede jackets and long colorful beads. One of my favorite things to do was play in her closet and dream up my glamorous future. As a child of the 60s my mother believed in spiritual phenomena and lived in a world of yellow submarines and pretty little daisies dancing in the breeze. I loved to visit her, go to work with her, and hang out in the "bunny" room where the Playboy "rabbits" were being measured for their costumes. Sometimes I would try on my mother's "bunny ears" or pull the "tail" of another bunny. Bodyguards protected the women from the unruly men who drank like fish.

My mother's jet-set lifestyle was in stark contrast to my life with my dad. Here, in Norco California, I spent my days riding Cricket, my Welsh Pinto pony, my best friend, in the hills beneath the trees and barrel racing in an open park. Cricket had white and tan spots and a wonderful personality. Sometimes we would ditch the saddle and ride bareback, as we loved the feeling of freedom. My other horses were great too but did not have Cricket's intelligence and sensitivity. My mother, who lived in Mexico with her boyfriend at the time, sent Cricket and me a red and black Mexican blanket and matching hackamore and reins. My pony and I thought we were very cool, and we were! No kid's horse had that Mexican flair.

I also had a goat, Penelope, and three dogs, Johnny, Travis and Critter, who were all older than me. From a young age my father had brought me up to be responsible: when one of the animals fell ill, it was my job to stay up all night and take care of it. On weekends and holidays my father took his wife, stepdaughter and me camping or snow skiing or waterskiing. My father's daughter, I was a daredevil and loved adventure! When we camped we slept in sleeping bags on a pile of leaves under a blanket of stars; the idea of a five star hotel was not even a glimmer. Hiding behind my fears was out of the question; my dad was a strict disciplinary and raised me to be fearless. He was strong and handsome and I loved watching him play baseball. He would slide into first base, his leg bleeding, but being the jock that he was he didn't care. He adored me and often made me feel like the best thing in the whole world, a queen. When he attended school stage-plays I was in he would stand up and yell, "That's my daughter! That's my Rochelle!"

Back in the 70s everybody drank. "The Martini" was a sign of elegance and sophistication, a most natural thing, and pretty much every adult I knew among my mother's and father's friends would sip on an evening cocktail. I was still a child but noticed that people could do strange things when they drank, and at times it made me nervous. I never knew what was going to happen next: will they be angry or nice? Most of all I felt left out. I had many wonderful holidays with my dad, holidays were important in my family, but I remember one special, little Christmas, with my mom. My mother and I were in her adobe house in Phoenix, across the driveway from the Hawaiian restaurant where she now worked. The parking lot I had to cross to get to the restaurant was like a thick carpet of crickets, especially in the summer when you had to walk, or run, for your life! Her adobe house was quaint, charming, full of love, but in the rainy season would flood and mud would cover the kitchen floor. I can still see my mom shaking her head and saying, "What a mess!" That Christmas, Mom bought and decorated a little Christmas tree and she treated me with candy, Bonnie Bell lip-gloss, bubble bath and Jean Nate perfume. She did not have a lot of money but spending Christmas with her was so special: I was with my mom – the one I thought did not want me! I understand now that it was not an absence of love for me; she was just too involved with her own life to be able to take care of me beyond a few holidays and vacations.

When I was nine my mother moved to Palm Springs, California, a 2-hour drive from where I lived with my dad. Sometimes on my visits I'd go with her to bars dressed up in adult clothes and dance with her men friends. Or we would go to pool parties and swim in gorgeous looking swimming pools. Indoors I saw white powder thinly lined on little mirrors. I did not know what it was and did not ask my mother or told her what I had seen; I just felt it was dangerous and wrong for a child to see stuff like that. If my father had known the kind of life I was leading when I was with my mother he would have never let me go visit her.

My mother was not stable. I would have friends come for sleepovers at my dad's house when one unfortunate phone call from my mother would bring the fun to a screeching halt. My friends and I would be gossiping or munching on good food or playing with my animals when the phone would ring and as soon as I would pick it up I'd know. My mother's tired, weak voice would come on saying – "I love you" – the code word for "I just took too many pills because suicide is the only answer."

I would have to decide, should I put down the phone and call 911, or should I stay on the phone because if I could hear her voice it meant she was alive. One time, after a suicide attempt, I visited her in the hospital. I was ten years old. She had been given charcoal to get the pill poisoning out of her body. As my mother was throwing up the charcoal and pills the nurses were looking down on her with dispassionate eyes. I stood in the corner of the hospital room in a state of shock. Why were they so mean to her? She had not tried to kill herself because her life was sheer joy; she was heartbroken after her lover had left her. Later in life I came to realize that my mother too had suffered in childhood from the trauma of abandonment. She had been the child of divorced parents, whose stepmother had separated her from her father. Every rejection by a man brought up her early trauma. For me, as a child, her suicide attempts were an abandonment of me. I was so afraid she would die and leave me for good.

In my teens my dad got a high paying job in computers in Colorado and we moved to Colorado Springs, a suburban town at the bottom of a valley surrounded by mountains. In this pristine beauty my life with my dad was rich with hiking trips 8,000 feet above the town, and cooking fresh coffee and pancakes on our campfire's open flames.

I was split between the two lifestyles. The country, wilderness and nature that made up my father's world and that of my mother that consisted of a roaring nightlife, high fashion and sex, drugs and rock n roll. When I was with my father I was a child, with my mother I was the grown up. In this confusion I made a decision to remain quiet and withdrawn. But sometimes I would be out of control crying inconsolably. Why was I so sad? No one asked.

My dad divorced his second wife when I was a junior in high school. My mother flew to Colorado to take care of me. It worked out that I was finally going to live my life's dream: I was going to live with my mother. But as my father was getting ready to drive Mom and me to the airport, and was carrying out my suitcases to the car in the driveway, all of a sudden my mother blurted out, "NO...I cannot have her live with me."

She got cold feet at the last minute. I was devastated. My father saw the expression on my face and demanded she fulfills her promise and take me with her. Finally she did. To this day my father regrets that decision and wonders what my life would have been like if I stayed with him. My mother continued to be unstable, each breakup from a lover followed by depression episodes and suicide attempts. I left her house and high school and followed my boyfriend to Los Angeles where I was penniless, rode buses, and stole peanut butter from my roommate.

Just like my mother, depression visited me and suicide called to me. In my late teens and young adulthood I chased men, chased one relationship after another. I needed to always have a boyfriend, be in love, high on the adrenaline rush of romance. The feeling of being wanted was an elixir of the Gods. It filled me with energy; I ate well, ran 12 miles every couple of days and slept well. I was happy. When a relationship was in jeopardy or ended I would become despondent, unable to face another day. I would close the drapes, as light scared me, and sink into bed, hiding. The worst was the day after my boyfriend left, realizing it's over. The pain of rejection and the fear of being alone paralyzed me; the only will I had left was the will to end it all. On a few occasions I took too many pills. Once, I slit my wrist. My boyfriend stood in the bathroom doorway laughing. He threw a towel over my wrist and called my father. "Come and get your daughter, she just slit her wrist."

From my diary
I've fallen into the abyss of depression. I am heavy and dead. Is J.M leaving me? I am swallowed up by fear. If he leaves me, my only answer is the grave.

I struggled with my emotions for a long time. One thing I knew about myself was that I liked to work. From age thirteen I had always had little jobs: I picked, cleaned and sold wild onions to our neighbors, I was a salesgirl in a clothing store and a hostess in a cafe. Now I searched the newspapers for a job and eventually responded to an ad and lucked out. The company sent a limo to take me to the airport, and after a short flight and short interview in which my natural talent to establish a good rapport with people was demonstrated, the CEO shook my hand, "You got the job!" It was a prestigious position in the legal department of a large corporation with a lucrative salary that allowed me to save a large sum of money. I married a French man, loved and was loved by his family that lived in France, and gave birth to our beautiful daughter. My life was stable and I felt good about myself. Except one day in a sales meeting, when I was asked to speak and teach other company employees what I had done to become so successful, I shrank into my chair. As I spoke I felt my voice returning to that of the injured and withdrawn little girl. I was filled with dread that I was doing it wrong, and that I would lose my job. After I finished my talk I turned to a colleague sitting next to me and asked, "Did I sound stupid?" Of course I had not, she responded. I had to adapt to the fact that I was far from stupid and had become the person I had always wanted to be, a strong tree that everyone could lean on, my family, friends, colleagues, everyone. Life was great. But not for too long...

My marriage that had started as a wonderful love affair, lost its Eros quality and became more like a brother sister liaison. The trips to France, the dress-up New Year parties and gourmet dinners prepared by my husband who was a chef, the theatre and movie outings were all replaced by an inexplicable feeling of anxiety and dread. From the outside, everything looked fine but inside I was vacant and alone. I could not explain this to my husband and felt I had to walk on eggshells so as not to disrupt the seemingly good life we were leading. I focused on taking care of my daughter and on making money. One day I knew I had to make a change. Frightening as it was, I filed for divorce.

My daughter and I kept the house. She was eight. Though life took a sling shot at me, our relationship kept me going. Every time I looked at her, all I could do was smile and take a deep breath. My blue-eyed, kindhearted, wise child was the utmost reward and greatest treasure I could have ever imagined. She still is.

I went on to date men and ended up with partners who were cheating on me and I had no idea. One final blow came in the form of a clean-cut, suit wearing, professional man. My daughter and I were living a stable comfortable life, owning multiple homes and having money in the bank. Everything was going well and then I lost it all. This man I was in love with and believed was perfect for me, was cheating on me too, and turned out to be physically and verbally abusive. Depression hit me hard and strong. I lost all my money – $100,000 of it to a charlatan card-reader who had promised to get me my lover back. She saw how desperate I was and took advantage of it. The "perfect man" saw how desperate I was and took advantage of it, sucking lots of money out of me. This was one of the darkest times in my life. I lost everything and had to start all over again.

By this time I had learned to meditate and visualize success and safety. I would sit on the sofa meditating, thanking the Universe that my electricity was still on, only to quickly be barraged by such thoughts as, shall I buy my daughter a roasted chicken or put gas in my car to drive her to school? My mother and father helped pay the bills and longtime friends stepped in to help.

Some of the money I had saved came from my hobby of buying and selling houses, but all but one of those houses had been lost.

It came down to selling my last house, in Lake Arrowhead, which I thought would be a short sale. Surprisingly I was lucky and made $200,000 on the sale. I paid everyone back and my daughter and I could breathe again. Unfortunately the sale was connected to a new man I was dating who helped me sell the house. He took $90,000 for himself. I had done it again: desperate to be loved, I bought myself a relationship.

From my diary
I don't know why but all the men I am attracting only remind me how unworthy, undeserving and stupid I am.

A few years passed. With the help of therapists and spiritual healing modalities I worked on myself to resolve my childhood trauma of abandonment. I began to see how this early experience had led me to chase men later on in life, and how the separation from them always brought me back to the experience of abandonment. It was a vicious circuit – I was recreating my childhood experience – as if on automatic.

When I met Michael, who is now my husband for many years, he introduced me to the University of Santa Monica (USM), where I earned my masters in Spiritual Psychology. This 2-year study program changed my life profoundly. It helped me get out of the chaos I had learned to live in. It taught me that our outer reality is a reflection of our inner reality and that changing our thoughts will change our life. It literally taught me to turn my outward pointing finger from my mom and dad and boyfriends and husband, and point it toward myself. Take responsibility for my life. It taught me that we are spiritual beings having a human experience. It taught me compassion and kindness.

Michael is from New Zealand and has lived and worked in many parts of the world. He is a "Renaissance Man" with a PhD in Philosophy with an emphasis in Depth Psychology, and possesses talents and expertise in design, art, digital architecture, social media marketing and writing. Michael is complex and bright and kind, and very generous: he cooks from scratch 8-course gourmet Holiday and Thanksgiving dinners for 25 people and more, taking up after his grandmother who had run an inn. I was attracted to how interesting, fun and different he was. My parents and Michael do not see eye to eye on many issues, and that, in addition to family quarrels with my teenage daughter, led to some conflict. Here I am again, I thought, I did it again, I attracted the wrong man into my life. But this time it's different. Michael and I have healthy communication skills and the good will to work through our problems. We are both practitioners in the healing arts and give self-empowerment courses and workshops together. We support each other in our creative, artistic and spiritual growth.

From my diary
I realize now that my "Dark Nights of the Soul" and all the emotional upheaval I went through as a child of divorced parents, and my failed marriage, and the painful breakups from lovers, and my suicide attempts – have all prepared me to be the healer and person I had always wanted to be.

I learnt that relationships do not determine who I am. Neither do the material things such as cars and nice houses. They are illusions to compensate for what we lack in childhood.

From my diary
I got a degree in Clinical Hypnotherapy and started giving sessions. I love my work, love to travel into the transpersonal realm where

soul and life meet; I love to help people, and it's easy for me to do. I am ready to open my own practice.

From my diary
My practice is booming! I have worked with thousands of people and was invited to speak about my work on television. I am beginning to write a book. I am on my way to enormous success.

From my diary
The more I work with clients, the more I see that life is like a seesaw: when we are up we feel as though the world is our oyster, we think we have all the answers, we are full of life and smiles. When we are down we are in the trenches of upset, operating in the lower realms of consciousness, attracting into our lives more of what we don't want. If we were to sit in the middle of the seesaw we would be in the neutral zone, which is our authentic, divine self – intuitive, peaceful, wise, kind and compassionate. Swaying on the seesaw from one side to the other we experience the illusions and projections on both sides, which can be uncomfortable and disorienting. Eventually we learn to return to center.

Healing is a journey not a one-time event or destination, healing means living life consciously, seeking meaning and purpose in the events of our lives. As much as I thought that I had learned all the lessons and mastered my life's curriculum, obstacles continued to show up on my path. After losing an extremely lucrative business due to the financial crisis, Michael had a stroke. Then our adventurous cat Miko went out into the street and was run over by a car. When Michael brought the dead cat into the house he was so broken, I feared he would have another stroke. Instead, unexpectedly, I suffered a rare brain malformation in the cerebellum that ruptured. Life radically changed. Starting with a complex six hour brain surgery, months of in-and-out of the hospital, ambulances, a spinal tap, multiple seizures and a prognosis that estimated years and years of recovery, brought me to my knees. As hard as it was to accept, as lost and broken as I was, something in me knew that if I manage to heal from this, I would be resolving the deeper layers of my abandonment issues – I was summoned to experience life's ultimate curriculum. It was demanded that I finally face and resolve what was still incomplete. Throughout the book I will interweave stories from my recovery, as well as case studies of my clients that show how the 7 *Paths to Healing your Relationship* and the principals of Spiritual Psychology and Clinical Hypnotherapy help us find our deepest selves and inner power, be in healthy relationships and experience harmonious lives that matter

CHAPTER TWO
THE STORY BOOK SYNDROME

We Don't Have to Be What We Were Taught.

Every client I have worked with suffers in one way or another from what I call the Story Book Syndrome. The story we see over and over on television and in magazines, in films, novels, fairytales, and in the lyrics to popular songs and operas that tells us what life is all about: we meet the object of our desire, fall in love, have babies, and live happily ever after. The books and movies and songs spin enchanting tales about the handsome, stoic knight riding his big white horse and carrying his princess away into the sunset. TV series and movies bombard us with romantic comedies where love conquers all, and spiritual teachers and gurus instruct us on how to find and keep our soul mate. Storybooks promise us that romance can be what we want it to be – perfect! At times, I too love to watch those sentimental movies that guarantee that the ups and downs in our relationship will be transformed by the "not so best kept secret" – that love is always grand!

The Story Book Syndrome encompasses an entire range of entertainment, amusement and theme parks where characters from worldwide known fairytales shake your hand and invite you to sit in their laps. These characters march and dance in parades and are the dream of every child to meet and be embraced by. These parks are a magical figment of the imagination where the sky is always blue, the grass is always green, and on a sunny Christmas Day in California it snows heavily, Halloween is a reality, and the fireworks that light up the sky fill us with immense excitement and exhilaration. These charmed stories with their bigger than life visuals and sounds, beyond the reach of one's reason and logic, impact a child's mind for a lifetime. My daughter had a season's pass to a fantasy park so she could live in the Neverland of promise and perfection where the good wins over evil and a prince will turn a toad into a pretty princess with the touch of a kiss.

I have wonderful memories of childhood experiences in such places that I will forever treasure. It is healthy to escape into glorious parks of mental freedom to balance the seriousness of life. In the US, visiting such theme and entertainment parks has become a family tradition that evokes lightheartedness and joy. In war zones, giant dolls from children's stories are brought in to play with traumatized children and comfort them. When taken with the right understanding, the fantasy world can nourish the imagination and inspire creativity. It can teach us what life is, and what it is not.

Where the fantasy world is dangerous and destructive is when there is no right understanding, and false expectations are created enslaving us to the idea that life is a Story Book, a vibrant theme park, a picture on the wall, and we wait for the prince's kiss to wake us up. We believe that our relationships will be as romantic and fantastic as those we see in the movies and on television. When they are not, we think that something is wrong with us. I see this in my clients all the time. So many of them believe it is their duty to marry and live such a fantasy-life. When the picture begins to crack, when one person "steps out of the frame," a tornado sweeps over the relationship and all hell breaks loose.

Because there is no Picture Book!

There are only concepts and ideas imposed on us by our families, society, community, friends, religions, culture, media, fashion – that take us away from ourselves until we no longer know who we are and want we want.

The Story Book Syndrome and Perfection

Our troubles become magnified and we criticize our lives that do not match up to the image of the Story Book. But perfection does not exist. It only exists in the Story Book. Compare yourself to the Story Book and you will always fall short. Try to have the relationship you've been brainwashed to believe you should have, and there will be only one outcome: you will fail! This is the Story Book Syndrome.

You are searching high and low to find the perfect mate who will offer you all that you've read in books and seen in the movies. You will never find it because it doesn't exist. But the minute you stop wanting and needing and looking and obsessing, and you take a deep breath and let life come to you in ways that you do not even predict or expect, the sooner you will find what you are looking for, and better.

We are all souls sharing a human experience. We come into this world – perfect in our imperfection – in order to evolve: to learn more compassion, more loving, more peace and harmony, we come in with the purpose to become more whole. The sooner we understand who we are, what our natural talents and gifts are and what our lessons are, the sooner we will find what we are searching for.

The processes in the *7-Paths to Healing your Relationship* will free you from the addiction to the Story Book Syndrome. You identify your particular version of the Story Book – the one you had bought into believing you must reach and become. That Story Book is imprinted in your subconscious since early on and is driving your life without you even knowing it. It is not what you really want; it is what others want for you. The Story Book constantly tells you what to do: marry a rich man, a doctor, or a humanitarian. Gain a degree before you get married. Make sure to wed your partner in case an out-of-wed-lock baby is expected. Endless Story Books and melodramas and we are flung into uncontrollable mood swings, jealousy, envy, fear and even hysteria.

The Seesaw

It is the Story Book syndrome that throws us from one side of the seesaw to the other. If we are on a date with a handsome and wonderful partner who happens to live in gorgeous villa, and to have a positive and spiritual outlook on life, and is also treating you sweetly and respectfully, then you are flung by the seesaw up high to the sky and you feel on top of the world. If it turns out that the person you've been in a relationship with is unemployed, letting you pay for every outing and has also been cheating on you, you have just been dunked down to the ground by the seesaw. You begin to doubt your self-worth, lose your self-confidence and blame yourself for having done something wrong. Life is such that we zigzag up and down, up and down, in relationships and in other areas, before we can find our seat in the center of the seesaw, the place of balance that supports our wellbeing and peaceful existence. After going up and down for a number of rounds, after differentiating ourselves from the Story Book we had thought our lives ought to be – what Carl Jung called "the individuation process" – then and only then are we able to stay for longer periods of time in our center. And when we lose our balance and are flung by the seesaw again, we know how to find our way back to center. Until then, be prepared for the stack of Story Book lessons. What is most important is how you relate to yourself in the process.

> *"The issue is not the issue, but how you relate to the issue is the issue,"* Dr. Ronald Hulnick, CEO of the University of Santa Monica.

If you are in a relationship, do the work in the relationship! Relationships are high spiritual work. As you diligently work on yourself and are true to yourself and your partner, you may realize that everything you've ever wanted is standing right in front of you. It's your own issues and irrational beliefs about relationships that have been blocking your view. Perhaps you have been lashing out at your partner, unconsciously and reactively like a Pavlov Dog. As you examine your own behavior and triggers, and you look into your childhood and other times in your life when you experienced trauma and suffering, you begin to understand the source of your current unhealthy behavior. You learn to heal those painful past memories, and you restore your ability to give and receive from a place of loving.

Each of our stories – our issues and our journeys of healing – is custom made and contains the exact lessons our individual souls need to learn. We are all different and none of us has to conform to what the Story Book is telling us. A novel, movie or the lyrics to a song may be inspiring, but they are not necessarily you. You have the freedom to carve out your own life – create and star in your own Story Book.

> *"You enter the forest at the darkest point, where there is no path. Where there is a way or path, it is someone else's path. You are not on your own path. If you follow someone else's way, you are not going to realize your potential."* — Joseph Campbell

When it comes to relationships there are lots of "dos" and "don'ts" emanating from the Story Book. For example, men grow up thinking that they must be the provider, be strong and hide their emotions. Sometimes women forget that men are human too. They do not have to be the only ones responsible for supporting the family and paying the bills. Boys have been taught that they shouldn't cry or show weakness. This is not true – boys, men, have as deep and as wide a pile of memories and dreams and insecurities as women do. You, Mr. So and So, do not have to ride the white horse and save your princess; you have the right to be *you* and choose how you wish to live your life. Do what is right for you; what makes you happy. As soon as you heal from your Story Book Syndrome – your false ideals and illusions about life and love – you will find the right mate. Whether you are a man or a woman, be kind to yourself and let go of the idea of the knight in shinning armor. It does not exist. It only exists in the Story Book.

Perfection is an inbuilt mechanism for failure. Those who seek the perfect mate, the perfect relationship, end up alone. Nothing is as you have been told it is, or should be. Nothing.

Seeking perfection lets you off the hook. You say, "If it's not perfect one, I don't want it at all," and you parachute yourself straight out of any possibility of a relationship. If you're not in a relationship, you don't have to confront your own shortcomings. It's easier this way, so you give up. This is not to say that one must be in a relationship, there are many single people who live fulfilling and happy lives. But if one wants to be in a relationship, it is crucial to take an honest look inside and heal the pain of the past.

CASE STUDY

One of my clients did not realize she was caught in the web of her family's tradition – the Story Book life that had been expected of her. Born in South East Asia where she lived till the age of twenty-five, she shared with me some wonderful stories about her culture and tradition, and then spoke the trauma. My client's parents were beyond themselves with anger because she refused to get married and came out to them as a lesbian. They were shocked and threatened to shun her from their world. They had their own version of The Story Book Syndrome. It was the traditional story that says that at a certain age a woman must marry a man, at all cost, even if it meant an arranged marriage. My client tried to fulfill these demands but she could not. However, her subconscious had been so totally programmed with the rules of her tradition that even when she stepped out of the box, and did not marry a man, she was drenched with guilt and could not find happiness.

My client and I worked hard until she was able to change her beliefs at the subconscious level. She learned to honor herself and her needs. She recognized that she only had one life to live, so why waste it? She studied her family's background and tradition and realized that her parents were projecting onto her what they had been taught. Her parents' relationship was extremely unhappy and unhealthy, but their tradition and beliefs ruled out separation or divorce. It had been an arranged marriage that should have never come to pass, as my client shared with me. Understanding her family's projections upon her, she felt relieved for she discovered the truth. My client loves her family but understands the dynamics imposed on them by their ancestors, religion and culture. She finally found the courage to honor herself and she married the woman she loved.

Stand tall and believe in what you want. We must live the life of our choice. We can treat others with compassion and respect but that does not mean that we have to give up our own happiness.

RECAP

In one way or another, at some point in our lives, we all suffer from what I call the Story Book Syndrome. From classical literature to popular media we are told enchanting stories about knights carrying their princesses into the sunset. Such perfection as displayed in the Story Book does not exist and only creates false expectations. No relationship is perfect. Every relationship requires work and this work starts with work on ourselves.

Inspirational Story

THE TROJAN HORSE

The Trojan Horse – a gift from the Greeks to the people of Troy – was a gigantic, hand crafted wooden horse, carved from pieces of natural wood that intertwined perfectly into each other. Much preparation, thought and skill went into its creation. When the majestic horse was rolled into the city of Troy, the Trojans received the gift with great jubilation. But in the midst of jubilation, a little door at the bottom of the wooden horse opened, and out marched the armed Greek soldiers who had been hidden inside and attacked the Trojans. The Trojan Horse was a trick.

One way or another as we reach to attain a goal, be it fortune, fame, success or love, we each create our own Trojan Horse – a disguising mask. This is an unconscious attempt to safeguard our souls, our deepest selves. We walk on this earth wearing our masks, playing our tricks on our lovers, bosses, business associates, friends, even on ourselves. We hide behind what we think we should be, wearing wigs, make-up and the latest fashion, driving Porsches and BMW's, our walls adorned with degrees and diplomas. We believe we must maintain the social status, the "hoopla," we were taught to think would make us accepted and validated.

The beautiful horse – the mask – enters the city of Troy – goes on a date, applies for a job, goes on an audition – and what happens? The truth comes out. Our hidden beliefs, our dark side, our insecurities, sensitivities, fears and false expectations all come out and the war begins. The mask has been shattered. Our thoughtfully constructed, beautiful but tricky horse falls apart. We are vulnerable, we are brought to our knees, we bottom out – reality stares us in the face. We can choose to run, hide or give up, or we can admit the falsehood of our mask, understand why and how we created it, and allow ourselves to be human; allow the parts of ourselves we have kept hidden to be revealed, healed and integrated. Unless we unlock the little door to our subconscious mind and disarm the "soldiers" that guard our soul, we will not be able to realize our full potential.

Our own Trojan Horse is the abode of our subconscious mind that envelops our soul.

THE WISDOM TRIANGLE

These are three areas for contemplation. You can write your thoughts, feelings, and responses on these pages or in your journal, or keep the contemplation in your mind as you go about your day and before you go to sleep. Your responses may change from day to day, and that is fine. So keep flexible, creative, courageous – and dare!

1. What was/is your Story Book Syndrome? What were you taught you should become?

....

....

....

....

2. Where did the illusion of the Story Book Syndrome lead you?

....

....

....

....

3. What's hidden inside your Trojan Horse?

....

....

....

....

CHAPTER THREE
CHAOS AS CATALYST

Through Life's Circumstances Our World Becomes Chaotic
Yet We Feel Comfortable in It.

magine you are lying on the grass in a beautiful green meadow watching clouds float by across a clear blue sky. In a moment though, your attention returns to the single flower in your hand and you tear, one petal at a time, and ask, in a mournful voice, "He/or she loves me? He/or she loves me not?" This is exactly the opposite of what you should be doing. Your wellbeing and happiness must not depend on the answer to this question; you can be independently happy regardless of its answer. Better to return to watching the blue sky.

Like nature, life cycles through seasons and after winter spring and summer always come. Winter can be so cold and dark that the arrival of warmth and light is often impossible to remember. "Winter" may be referred to as an emotional bottom: a time of gestation, of hibernation, like seeds deep in the soil under the ground. But the moment will come when the embryonic plant will emerge from the seed. For us humans it's at the bottom of the pit that we decide, "I cannot go down any further," change is necessary and nothing else. Like seeds that germinate in response to the correct amount of daylight, temperature and rainfall before a plant is ready to emerge, so to experience our spring and to bloom we must make a significant shift in our lives and work mindfully and diligently to create and sustain it.

The 7-Paths to Healing your Relationship guides clients through the darkness of winter, as I hold the light for you to emerge into the spring of your life.

The Chaos We Live In

We create the chaos we live in and have learned to feel comfortable in what we've created. It has become our comfort zone. For the alcoholic the comfort zone is the drink; for the cheater, his/or her concubine; for the abandoned child, as absurd as it sounds, chasing love and depression have become the comfort zone. Most of us live our lives completely unconscious of the chaos we live in, even when it is right in front of us. Our past is being projected into the future, becoming our "here and now." If in childhood our parents drank, chances are we will drink, thinking it is the normal thing to do. If our parents cheated on each other, we very well may continue the pattern in our own lives. If we suffered the pain of abandonment, we may repeat the pattern ingrained in us since childhood and attract people and situations into our lives in which we will be abandoned. It is also very likely that we will be the ones abandoning our husbands or lovers or children, as well as ourselves.

Our basic identity is formed in childhood and as adults we are still only grown up children reacting unconsciously and automatically to life's twists and turns. Our bodies may be in the present time but our minds operate off programs installed in it long ago that are no longer fitting the present situations. We march like robots, not seeing the reality in front of us, and instead we see pictures our minds were "programmed to read" back in childhood. In such chaotic circumstances, with the body in one decade and the mind in another, no wonder relationships end, and no wonder we fall apart.

The chaos we unconsciously create becomes our mirror and potent ground for healing and transformation.

Chaos is the cover, the "solution," to a deeper problem. I ask my clients to identify the chaos in their lives. Is it debt? Is it drinking? Is it jumping from one relationship to the next, from one job to the next?" I ask them about their childhood or prior life experiences that might be contributing to their current life style. They begin to make the connection between the present and the past. It is the beginning of the change. Often clients realize that how they perceived what had happened to them is different from what had actually taken place. Understanding the root cause of their chaos, clients are surprised and experience an "aha" moment followed by deeper peace.

I had a client who had been so depressed after her fiancé had left her she was on the way to jump off the Brooklyn Bridge. At that moment a friend offered her a drink. She took it and soon alcohol became her best friend. She felt comfortable in bars, she called drinking her "lifestyle," and only came to see me for hypnotherapy and healing when her life had become so chaotic she couldn't live like this one more day. She was failing her academic and creative classes in film school and she was fired from her jobs. I assisted her in recognizing that the drink was a cover to a deeper problem. She admitted that she drank to numb the pain, that the drink was "the solution," her coping mechanism. Exploring her childhood she identified abandonment incidents back then, chaos, and depression that ran down the generations on her mother's side. My client realized the chain of events: she had unconsciously recreated her sad childhood in the form a fiancé who left her, which brought her to drinking, which brought about the loss of her jobs and failing in film school, which brought her to me and the healing path! We worked deep on healing her childhood memories. She decided to forget her boyfriend and take her film school studies seriously. Soon she gave up drinking as making films filled her with satisfaction and self worth.

In chaos is the seed of creativity, in darkness the emergence of the light.

The Scars of Trauma

Each one of us has experienced at some point in our lives being in a pure and safe space. Even those who have lived in a war zone or with extremely abusive parents remember a particularly magnificent sunset, an unexpected birthday gift or a wonderful friend. But incidents of physical and emotional trauma have eroded those moments and replaced them with negative, self-destructive belief systems. By healing the deep scars that trauma leaves and learning to re-parent the sad, lonely inner child that still lives inside of us, we create a renewed safe space for us to live in. Since our deepest scars have gone underground into the unconsciousness, in order to heal we must uncover our subconscious mind and "reprogram" it to align with our new, self-honoring intentions.

You see, when we work with the conscious mind that contains our will power, reasoning and logic, we say, "I no longer want to eat the chocolate cake," or, "I want to stop attracting bad relationships." But the subconscious mind that contains its "library of associations" and all that we have learned and absorbed in and since childhood, says, "I love chocolate cake," or, "I am only worthy of abusive relationships." The subconscious mind will always win! It is much more powerful than the conscious mind. Hypnotherapy and the modalities the *7-Paths to Healing your Relationship* engage you in, bypass the conscious mind and go straight to the subconscious where healing on the deepest level occurs.

Trauma is the source of all addictions and failure in career and relationships. Only deep "reprogramming" of the subconscious mind will create long lasting results. Any other way, our addictions will surface the moment we are faced with a challenge.

Healing the Subconscious

Imagine a dreadfully entangled spool of wool. This is chaos. It will take patience to untangle the knots and courage to find and understand the connections between our chaos, trauma and lifestyle. But making some order in the chaos and learning a new way of thinking and of being, we step out into a glorious life filled with endless sunsets. Since the night is darkest just before the dawn, as the cliché tells us, the chaos in life resulting from trauma is an unavoidable stage and a catalyst for change that precedes the first stage of transformation. In depicting the Hero's Journey in his book *The Hero with a Thousand Faces*, Joseph Campbell named this stage "The Call to Action." He explains that when the hero/heroine are awakened from their unconscious and chaotic slumber, their first response is NO. Denial. The subject of the next chapter, the first path on the *7-Paths to Healing your Relationship*.

> *Until you make the unconscious conscious, it will direct your life and you will call it fate. – C.G. Jung*

RECAP

Our basic identity is formed in childhood and as adults we are still only grown up children reacting automatically and unconsciously to life's ups and downs. We unconsciously create the chaos we live in and this chaos becomes our comfort zone. Most of us refuse to recognize it as chaos, even when it stares us in the face. Spiritual psychology and hypnotherapy are effective healing modalities that reprogram the subconscious mind and get us out of living in chaos.

THE "BEFRIEND" MEDITATION

Find a safe and comfortable space to sit in ... Close your eyes, and allow all the chaos in your life to surface, like oil on water. One drop of chaos will catch your attention. Stay with it. Cry if you need to. Let it fill every pore of your body. Befriend the feeling ... befriend the chaos ... as unpleasant as it may feel. Don't be afraid, you are safe now... Let your mind take you wherever it wants to ... After some time you may feel a sense of relief. Notice what it is... name it and tell yourself what it is ... enjoy it ... put this new peaceful feeling in the space where chaos resided before. Write it down ... give thanks for it... let it lift your spirit and accompany you for the days to come...

THE WISDOM TRIANGLE

These are three areas for contemplation. You can write your thoughts, feelings, and responses on these pages or in your journal, or keep the contemplation in your mind as you go about your day and before you go to sleep. Your responses may change from day to day, and that is fine. So keep flexible, creative, courageous – and dare!

1. What chaos are you experiencing in your life?

....

....

....

....

2. What is the root cause of this chaos?

....

....

....

....

3. How would your life be if you turned your chaos into harmony?

....

....

....

....

Part 2

THE SOUL'S COACH – 7 PATHS TO HEALING YOUR RELATIONSHIP

Introduction to the Journey Ahead

O ur lives are the outcome of our thoughts; when we change our thinking our life will change. Our outer reality is a reflection of our inner reality – whatever is going on "out there" is a mirror that holds the key to our healing. The *7 Paths to Healing your Relationship* – Denial, Settling, Playing out, Acceptance, Intention, Spirituality and The New Story – is a guide and companion on the journey of healing.

But it is not a map to be followed step by step in order to reach the destination. It must not be understood as a linear process starting with Denial and followed progressively to the endpoint. It is rather a free, creative process that shapes itself differently for each one, and for some it *will be* a map to be followed with precision and exactness.

On *the 7 Paths to Healing your Relationship*, different people embark on the journey at different "ports." There are those who have been meditating for years but have not dealt with their emotional childhood crisis. There are those who can identify their trigger in a current situation and understand its source, but are unable to move forward into acceptance or commit to intentions that will turn their lives around.

Like the roots of a tree that are underground and unseen, the first three paths, Denial, Settling and Playing Out are on the subconscious level, and our task on the healing journey is to bring them to consciousness so we can move on and make cognizant, deliberate choices in our lives and relationships.

It is also important to know that you do not need to accomplish the successful navigation of all 7 *paths* in order to experience a change or transformation. The bricks on the wall-of-resistance-to-change will crumble one by one with each session, each contemplation, each meditation, gradually bringing a higher perspective, insight and wellbeing into your life. Nor must you be attached to any type of time or Chronos limitation. Different paths will take a different amount of time to traverse for different people. Healing is a process and is best viewed not as a ladder to climb but as a jigsaw puzzle with pieces falling into place allowing us to see and understand the connections between events in our lives.

Healing is a mystery, a dance between you, this book, your counselor, and especially the Great Spirit. So stay open and alert, and tune in so you can hear the guidance from within and without. This is an adventure of a lifetime in body and soul.

CHAPTER FOUR

Path One: Denial

If We Deny Our Problems
We Don't Have to Face the Music.

A bad thing happens. Our partner stands us up, speaks to us rudely, sets conditions that are too hard to fulfill, or, the worst, the partner leaves us. We are undone, traumatized, the rug has been pulled from underneath our feet. Yet, often at such times, we look the other way afraid to face the situation. No one likes to be belittled, or ignored, talked down to, cheated on, or have his/or her relationship break up. Looking deep within ourselves, or honestly and perceptively at our partner's behavior is too scary. Living in denial is easier. It allows us to avoid confronting the challenge – a challenge that could lead to a major breakthrough if we were brave enough to take the leap, or even a first step. How can we win victory over our challenges if we don't take the time and dare to look into our own behavior and how it affects the dynamic of the relationship? How can we maintain this relationship if we don't deal with the problems that threaten to end it?

DENIAL MANIFESTS IN A VARIETY OF BEHAVIORS AND ATTITUDES:

Are You Present?

Relationships are often compromised because we are obsessed with the past and all the traumatic experiences we have endured, and are convinced our future will be doomed as well. We live in the past with imagined fears about the future that create a false sense of reality and keep us from being present. We cannot see what's right in front of us because our childhood and formative negative experiences are getting in the way. Our minds are filled with worry and anxiety, since we are stretched all the way from the past to the future without any footing in the here and now.

The Endless Run

We spend our lives running because the moment we stop we feel how miserable we are, and that is unbearable. So we pretend to be happy, we pretend that drinking a lot is just fine, pretend we're okay with a cheating spouse. And when the ground is shaken we run in the opposite direction, hoping we'll never be caught and forced to deal with the problem. We think, "Those ugly green monsters will get me if I stop," and that often does happen. But when we dare to stop and become present and stare at what's in front of us without preconceived notions, those ugly green monsters melt like the Wicked Witch of the West in the *Wizard of Oz*. Then we no longer deny the problem by pointing the finger saying, "It's his issue" "It's the economy" "It's my childhood trauma" – non of which can be changed anyway – and we can see clearly what can be changed.

My mother used to tell me, "Rochelle, you can run but you cannot hide. You will always see yourself when you look in the mirror."

But most people refuse to look in the mirror and see what issues are "theirs." We end up living in the world of denial until we become stuck in a tiny little box with nowhere to go. Reality is forcing us to change, to grow beyond our perceived limitations. This is when most people seek help.

Whenever my phone rings I know that an injured soul is reaching out, ready to look in the mirror.

Looking the Other Way

It is a known fact that we will endure almost anything rather than change. Change is difficult. If your relationship has hit a wall and you don't enjoy or respect each other anymore, or if communication has dwindled or the Eros between you has died, it's important to look at it and deal with it – if you want to keep the relationship! There are two kinds of people: those who always take the blame for a problem at the expense of their own wellbeing, they are the doormat types, and those who always point the finger toward their partner in blame, with them it's always someone's else's fault. Whatever your pattern is, it has become your comfort zone. But sometimes, those of us who don't like to ruffle anyone's feathers, must take the risk and tell our partner, "You know what? What you just did was not okay with me!" At other times keeping yourself in check and taking personal responsibility for your part in the relationship problem is exactly what's called for. Often life forces us to leave our comfort zone in order to grow, this is just how life works! Unfortunately you'll find many relationships in which looking the other way has become the comfort zone, with neither partner's daring to leave it, until so much garbage has collected it's no longer possible to clean it up.

Recognize Your Triggers

We call "a trigger" something or someone that upsets you, that throws you off your horse, as we say. Back in your past there was an incident or event, small or large, that included words, actions, sights, smells and sounds that caused you deep upset, even trauma, and to this day when even a hint of a reminder of any of those elements is present, you react dramatically, unconsciously, and you may even experience a similar trauma – you have just been triggered!

Learning to identify your triggers is the key to healing. Triggers are the masters of disguise controlling your destiny. Think of a puppet and the puppeteer that controls the puppet. For as long as you do not recognize what your triggers are, your past is the puppeteer that controls your next move.

Triggers can spin you out of control and down the rabbit hole you go. More unhealthy thoughts are created in your mind that spiral you further out of control.

This is why it is important to address what is upsetting you. Identify your present trigger and ride its energy back to the earlier upsetting incident your trigger is reminding you of. You will understand the belief system you had created as a result. For example, one of my clients would become emotional and disturbed and turn her head away whenever she saw blood, especially in the context of war but even in a gory movie. Red blood was her trigger. In discussing her childhood she made the connection that as a little girl she had once combed her mother's hair and accidentally hit her in the eye with the pointy comb, and blood gushed out of her mother's eye. The little girl was hysterical, she felt guilty, and grew up into believing that whatever she did she always ended up hurting someone. In a relationship, she would be afraid to ask for her needs fearing that her request would hurt her lover. She did not feel worthy of having her needs met. In the hypnotherapy session my client released her belief that she had intentionally hurt her mother and that everything she did always ended up hurting someone. She learned to ask for her needs without being afraid. Today this client is a peace activist. She has turned "not wanting to hurt someone" to "wanting to help the world."

Identifying triggers is the first step out of denial. Work to conquer the belief behind the trigger, release the emotional charge you still carry as a result, and get on with your wonderful happy life!

The Here and Now

Until healed, the past will project itself all over the future. But the past is gone, the future is not here yet, and there is no other place and time to live in but here and now. What past have you been projecting onto your here and now? Is it a happy past full of cherished memories or is it trauma? Fear loves the past. It loves to destroy your present and assumes the worst for your future. Living in the past prevents you from being present to all that you are and can do and can have right now. It paralyzes you from taking your next step. Becoming present will help you out of denial and into admitting the problems in a relationship, or in life in general. Just because the past was painful does not mean that the present has to be painful too.

Many people see the world through the dark. Those who truly practice the here and now live in the light of freedom

Fear and Uncertainty

Fear gets in the way of everything. If you are like me, I can only imagine how many times you wanted to make a decision of some sort and fear stopped you. We only dare to engage in anything, relationship, job, travel, when we know the outcome will be pleasurable, profitable and successful. Uncertainty triggers the fear and disappointments we have learned to shelter ourselves from. I fought this battle over every decision I had to make. What I discovered is that fear is nothing but "chatter." It is made up of all the negative projections we have absorbed from everyone and everything around us through our lives. We had been so brain-washed that we came to believe that even the pain and suffering on television, films, books and musical lyrics are true, and that we too are doomed to experience drama, agony and conflict. Is it really so? NO, not at all!

Of course bad things do happen to people. I am still suffering from the brain surgery I had undergone some time ago. But I know that some day I will be completely recovered. And there is my work: no doubting is allowed to enter my mind. Not even the slightest doubt can creep into my conviction that I am headed toward complete recovery. Knowing it, affirming it, believing it, creates new possibilities. It affects the attitude with which I take the next step, and for as long as this step is taken in the "present," in the NOW, it can only have a positive effect on the future.

Buying into someone else's fearful projection, about illness, health or healing, will only take me down his/or her path, not mine. As my grandmother Cook used to say, "Half the stuff we worry about does not ever happen."

I remember a relationship I was in where I suspected that my lover was going to leave me. I was convinced that I was not good enough for him. I unconsciously projected my childhood fear of abandonment onto my counterpart, and presto I chased him away and he left. I created havoc where it did not belong. When I worked to heal my brokenness caused by the end of this relationship, I understood that my brokenness was but the symptom to the deeper and earlier root cause – my childhood abandonment – and it was that which I needed to heal, otherwise I would be continuing to recreate it.

Fear is the root cause behind unthinkable wars, ethnic cleansing, massacres and genocides on our planet. Fear is also the root cause behind domestic violence and all forms of assault and abuse within families and communities. Sometimes, if given a chance, people will request to right their wrongs, having realized they acted out of fear and made decisions they would normally not make. Fear is the evil driving force behind all pain and suffering. Fear is powerful. It is so powerful it is also behind such extraordinary acts of bravery as the mother who lifted the car off of her child. You have all heard it. The fear of losing her child filled her with super human power. This power is love.

Fear is the opposite of love.

Abandonment chases relationships. Having experienced abandonment in our formative years, it is likely that later on in life we attract relationships in which we feel triggered and threatened that we will be rejected and abandoned again. These relationships are our mirrors, forcing us to face and heal our earlier traumatic memories. When we let go of the hurts of the past, we are no longer afraid, and we stand in our authentic power attracting the right relationship into our lives.

Every person who shows up on your doorstep will mirror your wonderful characteristics as well as the flawed ones. Celebrate the former and work on the latter.

CASE STUDY

As a little girl, my client grew up with a father who had fought in the war and was suffering from PTSD. Often during dinner he would clear off the table in a fit of rage and demand that she and her mother leave the house. This happened on holidays too. On Christmas the mother would take her to a hotel and try to compensate for the father's behavior by buying her new clothes. They would bring a little Christmas tree to their hotel room and celebrate on their own. The mother desperately tried to make sure that her girl was okay. But sadly, the little girl always kept a packed suitcase next to her, knowing that everything was not okay. At home the little girl walked on eggshells to avoid her father's fits of rage. "You never knew when the yelling would start or you would be thrown out," my client shared with me.

Finally the mother took her little girl and left her husband. The little girl had to go to daycare where she was always the last to leave before going to stay for the rest of the day with a family that was paid to take care of her. At dinner the family ate in the dining room and the little girl was left in the front room, unfed, hungry, and impatiently waiting for her mother to pick her up. On their way home the mother would buy frozen dinners at minimarts, as she was too tired to cook for them. By the time the girl was five years old, she would be left alone in the house. She learned how to use the microwave and cook for herself by memorizing which numbers to push, as she did not know how to read yet. Often she was afraid to be alone. She grew up feeling bad about herself, unworthy and undeserving.

The little girl, my client, is now a young woman. She is beautiful inside and out, highly intelligent, successful, kind, and she wants to have love and a home. But feeling unworthy, all the men she had been dating in the past were all unavailable emotionally or otherwise, just like her parents had been. When she came to see me she was finally engaged to be married to a man she believed was the pot of gold at the end of the rainbow. But unfortunately he too turned out to be unkind. One Christmas, he was especially unkind to her and all her childhood memories of terror and fear and aloneness bubbled up to the surface. This time my client found the courage to face the situation and walk out.

My client identified holidays as her triggers. She learned how to dialogue with her inner child by going back to her young self and sooth and nurture it. I asked her: "What is your inner child telling you?" The inner little girl said, "I will never be alone again, I am safe, I have you and you have me! This is my true family."

My client is now on her way to finding the man of her dreams. She would never accept what she had to make do with as a child. She realized that there was nothing unworthy about her as a little girl, that it was her father's PTSD that terrorized the family. She realized that her mother had left her in daycare and with a family of strangers because she had no other choice, she had to put food on the table. She realized that in reaction to being terrorized by her father and seemingly abandoned by her mother, she internalized their patterns of behavior until she ended up terrorizing and abandoning herself. With hypnotherapy sessions and inner child work, she learned to properly "mother" herself and become her own family. Spiritually speaking, my client's "curriculum" – the lesson she had to learn – was to love herself and accept her life despite the curves and hardships that had been thrown at her.

RECAP

Living in denial allows us to avoid confronting our challenge, a challenge that could lead to a breakthrough. When bad things happen to us we are upset, traumatized, the rug has been pulled from underneath our feet, yet we look the other way, too afraid to face the situation. The only way out of this conundrum is to recognize what triggered it, and ride the energy back to a similar experience in our childhood that is the root cause of the present upset.

MEDITATION

Sit comfortably in a chair ... or you can lie down. Take 3 deep cleansing breaths.... Close your eyes and give yourself permission to sit quietly and just be.... Allow yourself to surrender into the surface beneath you. Sink calmly and soundlessly into the surface beneath you and allow yourself to relax deeply ... Imagine that you are in a beautiful place, peaceful, calm and quiet ... You see a colorful balloon. It can be any color you choose ... Next to you is a magic marker, and you write on the balloon ... D ... E ... N ... I ... A ... L ... "denial." You smile and release your balloon into the sky, and just like a child, you follow the balloon wherever it goes ... drifting and floating into the vast sky ... far, far away from you ... The balloon fades into the heavens, denial is gone. Anytime you think about denying something, you just imagine your balloon drifting and floating away from you.... Denial no longer holds your hand ... you are free.

THE WISDOM TRIANGLE

These are three areas for contemplation. You can write your thoughts, feelings, and responses on these pages or in your journal, or keep the contemplation in your mind as you go about your day and before you go to sleep. Your responses may change from day to day, and that is fine. So keep flexible, creative, courageous – and dare!

1. What are you denying – what don't you want to look at?

....

....

....

....

2. What kind of behaviors have your denial led you to?

....

....

....

....

3. How would your life be if you faced that which you are denying?

....

....

....

....

CHAPTER 5
PATH TWO: SETTLLING

I Am Not Good Enough for a Better Relationship,
so I'll Settle for This One, Even Though I Am Not Happy in It.

We settle into relationships that are unsatisfying, unhealthy, even dangerous, because we are afraid to be alone. We settle because we do not want to lose our children or our money in a divorce. So many of my clients would have liked to uncouple but are afraid to do so. It is easier to settle, to look the other way. Let us not rock the boat. It is safer to stay with what we know. Fear of the unknown is eclipsing our thinking. We have been taught since childhood that being alone is bad. It says so in Genesis: "It is not good for the man to be alone; I will make him a helper suitable for him." Being married or in a long-term relationship is the respectable position in our society, and has been so for millennia. One is measured by one's marital status. We fear losing that respect, that status. We bargain with ourselves, we justify, we make up every excuse we can think of to stay in the marriage, in the relationship, and so, slowly and without noticing, we have settled into misery.

Or think about arranged marriages, the type of marital union in which the bride and groom are selected by their families. The parents answer to their culture's demands, the children settle for the arrangement whether they like it or not, and the pattern continues from generation to generation. What about being with the *right person* who will add sunshine into your life? In many instances not enough emphasis is placed on this component, call it love, understanding, compatibility. I would rather be alone than settle. But there was a time in my life I would have not said that, a time when my inner child was still running my relationships, forcing me into the shame and pain of settling for less before I could recognize my worth, know what I really wanted and make self-honoring choices.

The Inner Child

Our inner child is creative, imaginative, adorable and innocent. Unfortunately, it is also the part in us that was hurt in childhood, and the wounds are still bleeding. Until we heal this part, we are all children living in an adult body. Our inner child is unconsciously running our adult behaviors and reactions. What we experienced as children we have become. As we move through each of the *7-Paths to Healing your Relationship* program, you will identify the voice of your inner child and listen to what he/or she has to tell you. Allow the child to speak freely, and uncover what it is afraid of. When your inner child is heard, your adult self can re-parent it, making it feel safe. I call this *safe work*. You will find that after your inner child is healed, your adult self will experience the freedom you seek.

As children, we took on problems in our families as if they were our own. When parents divorce, or when a mother or father has to leave a child behind in order to make a living, the child will often think it is his/or her fault that created the separation. The child feels abandoned and responsible. Parents don't always explain the circumstances to their children in a way the child will understand that it is not its fault. The child is not told that it doesn't need to bear the responsibility, or fix, or even help the parents in their adult problems. The parent is the rock for the child, and when the rock is shattered the child will take on the responsibility and the guilt for it, and later on in life will settle into situations and relationships that are similarly painful.

Understanding how our own disrupted early life affects our present, we have the opportunity and the duty to help our own children process life's circumstances in a healthy way, so their inner children will not run their lives in the future.

Recognize Your Inner Child's Triggers

Look at what upsets and causes you to react in a negative way. It is usually something carried into adulthood from the past. What was your experience as a child that is begging to this day to be heard, understood and healed? What conclusions and decisions have you derived from your traumatic childhood experiences about the world and about yourself? Can you locate one or two disturbing incidents in time and place? Becoming aware of the events in our formative years that shaped us is crucial to healing.

Maybe you heard your mother call your father names and you began to think that all men are cruel and insensitive. Maybe when you were a kid someone told you that you are not pretty, or are too fat, or stupid, and you bought into it. Now in your adult life, when you suspect that someone perceives you as not pretty, or too fat, or stupid, your inner child will force you into believing it. You will become depressed, fall ill, end your relationship, or, in so many cases, cling to a dying and harmful relationship.

Listen to and Re-parent Your Inner Child

Our inner child desperately wants to be approved of and loved. One of my clients came to me seeking help on how to hold on to the relationship she was in. All her previous relationships had ended with her partners leaving her, and she did not want this pattern repeated. When I asked her about her childhood she told me that often when she had tried to speak to her father about an upset she had had with a friend, he would rage and tell her: "Just don't show yourself to anyone. When they really know you, they will leave you." My client's "logical" conclusion from his words was that she was not good enough for anyone to love her. In her previous relationships, still hearing her father's voice in her head, she would become deeply insecure and unconsciously lash out at her partner, causing him to leave her.

In our sessions she began to re-parent the inner child. We discovered that as a child she loved to draw and had an ear for music. I suggested she spend a few hours a week drawing. She started singing in a small choir, too. I gave her an exercise, to put a rubber band on her wrist and every time she felt insecure, instead of lashing out, snap the rubber band and remind herself, "I am not my father, and I don't have to rage like he used to." At night, before going to bed, I advised her to hold her imaginary little girl in her arms and speak to her: "Don't be afraid, little one, I am here for you – I love you." My client practiced inner child work on a constant basis, and she loved it so much, she still practices it. You see, inner child work is a life long process and becomes second nature to us. In my client's case, she placed a few childhood photos of herself around the house and when she passes by them she sends love to the little girl. And she plays music loudly and dances to it, something she had never been allowed to do as a little girl. This lady in now happily engaged to the man she loves and who loves her. Don't ever underestimate the power of inner child work!

Assure the inner child that it will never be invalidated; give it what he/or she was deprived of, tell this precious being, "I love you!"

The Voice of Abandonment

Children who suffer from the pain of abandonment want to be loved and approved of, and they continue to search for it their entire lives. "I am desperate for love," "I am not good enough," I am unworthy." Sounds familiar? When as adults their partner leaves them or rejects their love, they experience once again the excruciating pain of abandonment, as painful as it felt in childhood. Those of you who experienced some form of abandonment in childhood, extreme or subtle, it is important to learn to love yourself first. Like my client did, give your inner child now, what it did not receive in childhood. Maybe it's a cone of strawberry ice cream, a night at the circus, or a box of pastel colors you so yearned for as a kid but Mom had no money to buy it for you. Teach your inner child that it is possible to walk in grace, and that life will not always fail you.

We've all experienced being bombarded by unstoppable negative thoughts all day and night long. This negative chatter gets in the way of our healthy and creative thoughts, and opens the door to an avalanche of fearful beliefs, feelings and behaviors. This, in many cases, is the result of the inner child not being heard. When you hear these negative thoughts – the voice of your inner child – listen, acknowledge its pain and fear, speak to it calmly and lovingly, and free your inner child and yourself from the endless slavery of unhealed childhood trauma.

Why Settle?

Fear. I tell my clients to stop, take a deep breath, and ask the deepest voice inside of them what they should do. I tell them to listen for the answer without judging, evaluating or negating it. After a moment their eyes moist up, vulnerability shows on their faces, as they hear the voice of depression, anxiety, shame, dread, – the full range of painful feelings they have been pushing down. I explain: "These feelings are trying to get your attention that something is wrong and they want you to do something about it." The clients will often come back with the realization that they have been settling for lives or relationships they are not happy about.

It's time to take care of yourself! Animals go into a quiet corner and lick their wounds, nurturing themselves. Having realized that you are settling for a life or a relationship that is "less than" what you want or deserve, you may want to take a step back and search for the lesson you are being asked to face. Be kind to yourself. Again, ask yourself, what does the inner child has to tell you? Where did you learn that settling is okay? When did you begin to think: "I am not good enough for a healthy relationship, so I'll just settle for this one, even though I am not happy in it."

What is Projection?

A projection is a disowned and unrecognized characteristic within ourselves that we attach to someone else. When we refuse to recognize a particular characteristic or behavior in ourselves, life will present us with a person who embodies that characteristic and behavior. If, for example, a man does not own his sensitive and emotional nature, he will meet a person, maybe be in a relationship with a partner, who is emotional and sensitive – and he will hate it! Until he recognizes and owns these qualities in himself! This is called a negative projection. There are also positive projections, such as the admiration of a teacher or a movie star. When we do not own and recognize our own teacher-like, or star-like quality, we see and admire it in another. We can learn from both negative and positive projections what we need to heal in ourselves, what our potential is, and how we can grow.

We must recognize our projections before we can change our negative thoughts and beliefs. Like cobwebs hiding in the attic – you don't know they are there until you go up and look. As cobwebs will take over the attic if not cleaned out, so our negative thoughts and beliefs will take over our lives and make us miserable if we don't reframe them.

Whether trying to solve relationship issues, weight loss, or any other issue, you'll discover that your belief systems are based on your past. The past has become your identity. To resolve an issue is to identify the pain of the past that created the belief system, heal it, and replace it with a new and constructive way of thinking. If you listen carefully, you will perceive how someone is seeing the world. You will perceive their past through a transparent present. For instance, if someone tells you that he/or she will die if you leave them, it most likely means they have abandonment issues. Belief systems established in our formative years are created by what we learn from our families, teachers, friends, religion, media and the culture at large. These beliefs construct who we are for the rest of our lives, and will not change on their own; we must work consciously and diligently to update them. Ask yourself, "What do I believe?" We project the beliefs learned in childhood into our present and future, but do these beliefs still hold true today? Most likely not!

Those of you who suffered trauma may experience a life tainted by feelings of fear, guilt, rage, shame and resentment. Those who were abandoned in childhood will be in fear that their partner will leave them. They will be constantly on guard, unconsciously sabotaging the relationship and inadvertently causing their lover to leave them, thus recreating the childhood experience. Beliefs we learned early on in life do not hold true today, but the subconscious mind, thinking that they do, will continue to run them until these beliefs are updated.

Relationships are fertile ground for old beliefs to sprout in, creating pain and havoc. But relationships are also the space in which to heal and change these old beliefs, and "test" them.

The future is an illusion. We have no idea what is going to happen. Most of the time, the here and now is perfectly fine. As my grandmother used to say: "Rochelle, not everything you worry about is going to happen." Indeed not everything we worry about ever happens, unless we make it happen. If we project our past into the future, our present becomes a mess. But if, instead, we understand the past and the causes of our trauma and suffering, and we do the inner work to clear and heal it, we become freed from the antiquated belief systems of the past.

Often we react to a situation as if it were a past experience and not the here and now. I used to be constantly afraid that a man I was in relationship with was going to leave me because "I'm not good enough." In childhood I had been wanted and loved by my parents, but following their divorce when I was five years old, I felt abandoned by my mother. My mother too had suffered from abandonment in her childhood, and when one of her lovers left her she would fall into a debilitating depression and try to kill herself. On many occasions I witnessed this and felt responsible: if she died it would have been my fault – I had not been able to keep her alive. These experiences were the basis of my early life. I did not feel safe, yet had to be the adult. My mother could not take care of me because she had her own issues, but as a child I did not understand this and thought that she did not want me. I was afraid she would leave me, I was afraid she would die. As an adult I continued to fear, "I am unworthy of a man staying with me. He will leave me, the relationship will end." So even when I was in a destructive relationship, I settled for it, letting it be what it was without asking for my needs, without asking to change anything, afraid that if I rocked the boat my partner would leave me and I would be left alone.

Abandonment takes many forms. My experience was that of a child of divorced parents and a mother who attempted suicide a number of times. Others had different experiences: a handicapped child was an outcast in school, another had to sleep under the railroad tracks to hide from Child Services, yet another was looked down on for being of a different race or religion. In essence there is a common denominator to all of these: the child felt isolated, alone, ashamed, and in fear of being separated and deprived. I have worked with many such cases. My own childhood experience and my empathy help me support these clients to re-establish a feeling of self-worth and confidence, reconnect to life, and find a sense of belonging.

Identifying Your Projections

Life is one big projection. We project our belief systems onto everything and everyone. We are what we have been taught, some of our teachers were empowering and others disabling. Understanding this is key to a healthy personal and relationship life. We have learned most everything we think and do by watching others behave in the ways that they had learned in their past. If we saw aggression and violence, we would often repeat the pattern, as either victim or perpetrator. It is a vicious circle. In relationships we project our beliefs onto the other person. In my office I often hear, "It's my way or the highway." But everything does not have to be just one way! What about being flexible and letting go of the way you think it ought to be, and listen to what your partner wants? What about asking yourself what you want? Are you being heard? Are your needs being met? It works both ways. The key word is "listen." Get out of your own way and listen to what the other person is trying to tell you. Listen to what your own inner child is trying to tell you. This calls for alert and attentive listening, as when searching for truffles in a forest. Some truffles are poisonous and others are good to take home and eat, and we must carefully distinguish between the two kinds.

Same in a relationship: you are seeing and experiencing everything through your own filtered perception, so be attentive, clean the lens, and be careful which "truffle you take home." As you examine your own world first, and identify your beliefs and triggers, you will see how everything changes. You will be shocked to discover how worthy you are by just being you! Your partner will finally be heard, and the two of you, rather than fight and react defensively, will find ways to communicate consciously and openly. Most of all, you will no longer be the victim of your past pain creeping in.

CASE STUDY

I coached a couple. The wife came from a destructive, violent family. She always felt she had to be the strong and courageous one so as to keep some sense of control over what was going on around her. This was her way to feel safe. Later in life she projected her control issues onto her children and husband. They were so overwhelmed by her obsessive controlling behavior that they started to lash out back at her, which made her even more controlling. Everyone was upset – the children, the wife, and especially the husband.

The husband came from severe poverty, which left him feeling inadequate. His mother had been the domineering type and controlled her son and her husband. My client's father, full of shame, had retreated into his "cave" and hid from the critical eye of his wife and son. As a result, my client hates being controlled and yet he married "his mother" in the form of an equally controlling wife.

Initially, when my client and his wife had met, they were comfortable with each other. The husband had helped the wife feel safe by protecting her, and only once in a while had been exposed to her controlling outbursts. The wife had helped her husband in business and he became the success he had always wanted and knew he could be. But as years went by, the wife's control issues shot through the roof. The husband – like his father before him – retreated into a "cave," only his cave was the bottle of bourbon. Having married "his mother," my client became "his father." This was a problem and caused the couple to lose control of their marriage. The children knew that something was wrong.

As we started working together, the couple decided to live in separate homes for a period of time so they could each heal on their own. They worked separately on themselves, each understanding their past. The wife understood that she had survived in her abusive family of origin by controlling her world, but that she no longer needed to be controlling; her world was now safe. The husband understood that the seeds to his overuse of alcohol had been planted in his poverty-stricken childhood, with a domineering mother and a fearful father who drank. The husband and wife realized that they did not have to carry these patterns into the present. They healed the past. They are both healthy and living back together in peace. The wife learned how to control herself and not her family. She learned to allow others to be free and experience their own life lessons. The husband stopped drinking and learned to take back his power. He no longer needs to live in the "cave of giving up and shame." He has the right to speak out and be heard. The children are happier. The family has been restored.

RECAP

We settle into an unhealthy and unhappy relationship because leaving it is too frightening, we'd be pitted against an unknown future that could be even worse. So we take what we can get and hold on to damaging situations. If we track this pattern back to an earlier time in our lives, we'll discover that somewhere in our formative years we experienced pain and trauma from which we concluded that we were unworthy and undeserving of a better life. That conclusion is ingrained in our subconscious and still calling the shots. But with inner child work and by identifying our projections it is possible to mend the wounds of the past, to recognize our worth, and find the strength of heart to move forward toward the life and relationship we seek.

Inspirational Story
THE LITTLE TRUFLE

In France one afternoon a week, my daughter and I, my former husband, and his mother who we called Maman, would accompany Papa, my father in law, on a "truffle hunt" in the forest. With each and every step Papa would carefully search for the one little good truffle that might be peeking out from the ground. We had to be alert and calm and present, like in a walking meditation. Picking up a poisonous truffle could have resulted in a tragedy.

The trees protected us from the sun, you could hear the laughter of children playing hide and seek somewhere in the forest, and birds danced and serenaded us as we quietly searched for our delectable treats. When Papa would find his diamond in the rough he would sigh ah... ah.... with a big smile on his face... He would kneel, brush the soil off his long lost friend with a tender gesture before plucking it, and with delicate fingers wrap the little morsel in his cloth and place it in his basket. It was as serene and peaceful an activity as a Zen Tea Ceremony.

The truffle hunt with Papa inspired me to see beauty in ordinary life. It taught me to be present to such moments. When we are present with ourselves, the past is just the past. We no longer live in the box of "stuck" thinking. We no longer remain entrenched with our past beliefs that spill out into our lives. Relationships require tenderness and care – like looking for delicate truffles in a forest. They require being alert and paying attention. When looking for truffles we are careful not to step on them and not pick a poisonous one. So it is in relationship. We must be careful whom we pick; we must be careful not to step on each other's toes, as we all have delicate parts inside of us; we are all little truffles.

To find your truffles you must become present

MEDITATION

Sit back and relax, take a few long, slow, deep breaths ... Close your eyes and imagine that you are on a calm and quiet beach ... take another deep breath ... notice the weather, what is it like? ... What kind of sand do you see? What is its color and texture? Keep walking towards the water.... listen to the waves rolling in and rolling out, rolling in and rolling out, rolling in and rolling out ...

Allow the waves to echo your breath, breathing in and breathing out, breathing in and breathing out ... you are so calm.........

As you walk slowly to the shoreline you notice an island ... you look at the island and notice a person walking on it ... Beside you on the sand is a magical pair of golden binoculars, you look into this binoculars and see that the other person on the island is you, yes, you. You watch yourself.... what are you doing? Who have you become? You notice that you are no longer settling. Your face is full of peace and you are happy.... You are honoring and respecting yourself for who you are. You are grateful... your world is exactly the way you want it to be. You put down the binoculars and decide to swim to "Freedom Island," ... but, the water is rough ... you see scary fins in the freezing cold water, so afraid to swim, you plant your feet firmly in the sand beneath you ... As you take another deep breath you decide to take one more look into your golden binoculars and ... your eyes meet ... your peaceful self smiles graciously back at you ... and with open arms invites you to swim "*home*." ... You take another long, very deep breath ... again you look at the water, it is calm and warm now, the island is very close, and the fins are dolphins playing like children waiting for you so they can help you swim to your place of freedom.... They are there to guide you. You feel safe and take the final plunge. You swim toward Freedom Island ... your Higher Self. You no longer fear, you no longer settle for what you don't want, you now live in your new world. You are at peace.

THE WISDOM TRIANGLE

These are three areas for contemplation. You can write your thoughts, feelings, and responses on these pages or in your journal, or keep the contemplation in your mind as you go about your day and before you go to sleep. Your responses may change from day to day, and that is fine. So keep flexible, creative, courageous – and dare!

1. What have you settled for?

....

....

....

....

2. What are you afraid of and why?

....

....

....

....

3. How would your life be if you didn't settle?

....

....

....

....

CHAPTER SIX
Path Three: Playing Out

Our Behaviors Reflect Our Hidden Wounds
Asking to Be Healed.

Harmful behaviors we unconsciously play out will eventually force us to face our issues. A woman with a marijuana smoking habit loses job after job; a gambler ruins his family burying, them in debt; a couple fights tooth and nail with each other. When did all this start and why? How will these individuals rise up from the troubles they have fallen into? These behaviors can be seen as tragic and unsolvable, or as the cry of their emotional wounds hidden in the subconscious that will turn them toward healing and transformation.

Let's examine the case of the couple that fights tooth and nail. They trigger each other with the simplest of things, like not making the bed or leaving dirty dishes in the sink. Quickly an argument ensues and escalates to verbal abuse, name-calling, blaming, a hitting, a slammed door, and worse. Sadly, what's happening is that both spouses have not yet healed their own issues and are projecting their "shadow material" – their deep wounds they are not aware of – onto each other. The husband is upset with the wife for not making the bed. In his childhood he was forced by his Marine father to make the bed in the military fashion, and has never forgotten or gotten over the beatings he received from him when the bed had not been properly made. He has never forgiven his father for the rigid upbringing forced upon him as a boy. When the wife does not make the bed, as she promised, it triggers the husband's childhood memory hidden in the subconscious, and a simple thing like an unmade bed causes him to play out and direct his buried anger at his father toward his wife. The wife grew up with a mother who worked nights and would leave the dirty dinner dishes in the sink. When the little girl would wake up in the morning – the mother was still asleep – she could not find one clean glass to pour herself a glass of milk. Now, when she enters the kitchen and sees that her husband did not wash the dirty dishes, as he had promised, her childhood memories of neglect are triggered and she lashes out at him. Both make an elephant out of an anthill. What is needed is for both parties to take the time and clarify and heal their own childhood wounds so they would no longer project their shadow material onto their partner. The relationship would then take a turn for the best. Things would look very different.

Playing Out is a Symptom to a Deeper Problem

Many parents abuse their children physically and verbally and find it justifiable. Such behavior stems from their unhealed childhood trauma. Most likely they have experienced such behavior at the hand of their own parents, who also found beating their kids justifiable. The shame and humiliation, the extreme fear at the mere sound of a father's unbuckling belt or the sight of a mother's raised hand got imprinted into the "library of associations" in their subconscious mind – and are now unleashed onto their child. The behavior of those who raise a hand on their kids or invalidate them in any way is but a symptom to the deeper problem. Only when they heal their own emotional wound will they no longer play it out unconsciously and viciously toward their children. There is no justification for violence against children. If parents would seek help and explore their own childhood, they would remember, heal, and forgive the pain that had been inflicted on them by their parents. They would learn to overcome their reactive, violent nature and replace it with peaceful modes of communication, with alternate ways of educating their offsprings. Often those who beat up their children find war and violence and extreme police measures justifiable also. If we want a more peaceful world, it's time to find the root causes of our own destructive behaviors toward ourselves and others. "Peace begins with me," goes the saying.

Those of you who are willing to explore past lives may find the root of your behaviors and attitudes in the lives prior to this one. Hypnotherapy can lead you on a journey of discovery deep within your subconscious where all memories are stored, and where you may find answers to the larger problems. A woman who is constantly on the defensive may discover that in Roman times she had been tied to the back of a carriage and dragged around town, and to this day she holds in her psyche fear, humiliation, trauma and the need to defend herself. Now that she found and healed the source of her defensiveness she may start to feel safer in this world without needing to shield herself. A gambler, putting his family in harm's way, may discover that in a past life he had suffered great poverty. A barren woman may discover an early life in which she had witnessed the killing of her child and will do anything – including becoming infertile – to never experience such horror again.

Every Upset is an Opportunity to Learn and Heal

Once you understand the root causes of your trials and tribulations, you start making your way up into a more peaceful mind. That which has been throwing you into an uncontrollable tantrum, from this or another lifetime, can now roll off your back like water off a rock. The more we clear our minds of its shadow material, the more peaceful our minds will become. A peaceful life will follow a peaceful mind. Some will call this a state of enlightenment, nirvana, or satori, to name a few options. To reach this state we must first do the psychological work: feel, understand, reframe, and change our thinking. As the saying goes: we become enlightened by shedding light on the darkness.

With a peaceful and centered state of mind, devoid of self-criticism and rooted in your authentic power, it will be easier for you to attract the life and relationship you desire.

Your addictive and destructive behaviors are here to call you to change. They are the logs to be burned in the fire of your emotional healing and spiritual transformation. As you work on resolving your issues, watch those logs being burned to ashes and taken into the upper realms to be transmuted into love, peace and harmony.

Chasing Love

You do not need anyone in order to be whole – you are already whole. The road to a wonderful relationship starts with you. Working through your issues you will first and foremost build a loving relationship with yourself; you will become secure in yourself and will no longer need anyone else to validate you for who you are. You will know who you are. This will require some rigorous honesty since lying to ourselves is easy, and one of the wildest demons to conquer.

Make yourself whole first. Expressions such as "she is my better half" romanticize an illusion, for a relationship between two "halves" is doomed to fail. When you're whole in yourself and rest in that knowing, you will no longer chase someone else to fill in the lack you feel inside.

I remember the heartache of constantly searching outside myself for love. If someone loved me that meant I was okay because they validated me. If the person did not love me, that was it. I would march myself right back into the trashcan of pain and sorrow. Again and again I played out my unworthiness card and proved to myself that I did not deserve to be loved. I spent my life chasing one unhealthy relationship to another, and the cycle continued until my life spiraled out of control. This "out of control" was my way of playing out my out of control childhood experiences, and my ensuing sense of unworthiness.

When a therapist asked me: "What would happen if you sat in your chair and allowed someone to come to you," I thought she was speaking Chinese! Because I believed that no one would ever come to me.

What I identified as "love" included abuse and abandonment. This is what I knew and felt comfortable in. What the French call "Malade D'amour" – "sick with love." In all relationships, but mostly those with men, I was called stupid, wrong, and a terrible person. I was yelled at, physically hit and threatened. The more inadequate and humiliated I was made to feel, the more I needed my lovers' love and approval, the more I went out of my way to please them. For that little bit of love I would sell my soul. My life could have been produced into a Soap Opera, and I am sure many of yours could too.

News flash! You can't buy love.

I was constantly chasing. I was addicted to the chase, and my chase never brought me anywhere. It was a miserable life. If the relationship was in trouble I was panic-stricken, "He is going to leave me." Once, to avoid this, I bought a very expensive surfboard and had it delivered to my lover's door. If you have to do this, stop and take a look in the mirror, something is drastically wrong! Money, or your physical appearance, will not buy you love. Paying a psychic who promised to bring my love back $100,000 is crazy thinking, but I did it. The psychic made out great. The client – me – lost a lot of money. Yep. You can't buy love and no one can get a person back!

The only person you can "get back" is you, because the truth is that you never lost it, you just forgot. Reweave your safety net of validation and you'll remember.

Childhood trauma and the grief over loss do not vanish with the passage of time, nor are they "forgotten," as many parents tend to think. The adult self holds on tightly, although unconsciously, to the childhood experience and plays it out in the present. What happens in the mind of a child who is the victim of rape or violence, sexual or emotional abuse, poverty, or the loss of a parent or sibling? In such moments of deep vulnerability the child's mind will make irrational decisions and come to believe them: "I am not good enough" "I deserve it" "It's because of me." These irrational beliefs hide the original trauma and are carried into adulthood and played out. For example, if a child lost his parents in a boat accident, he/or she may be afraid later in life to go on a boat trip with a lover. The past governs our psyche. We react in the present as if the past has never ended. The truth is, the past does not end – until we say it ends!

Here too, inner child work will be beneficial. Wrap your arms around your inner child and say: "I promise you, little one, that you will never be left alone again. Love and safety will find you because you are love, and for that very reason you will attract love. It's different now, you always have ME, the grown you. You do not need anyone to make you feel safe or loved – because you have me."

For those of you who were blessed to enjoy a happy childhood but still struggle with relationships, please keep reading. Your outer reality is a reflection of your inner reality. What are your beliefs that play out in your life?

Feelings Are Not Facts

They may seem to be, but most of the time they are just old memories imprinted on our "emotional body" that are being triggered in the present time, creating upset feelings. When you are triggered, try to look clearly and concretely at what is in front of you. Label it for yourself. For example: "I just read a poem I wrote to my friend, and she just raised an eyebrow and asked for more sugar in her tea." Then tell yourself how you feel about it: "I feel invalidated and unseen." Then rather than blaming her for having invalidated or not seen you, know that "your school is in session." How you feel now has happened before. Track back and find that incident. Heal it, reframe it, and return to the here and now. This is the theory behind "I am upset because..." Because my husband did this, my child did not do that, the war, the economy, the boss... etc. All this may be true, but it's not going to heal you. You will just stumble deeper into the abyss of blame. But if, when something upsets you, instead of pointing the finger out you turn it inward and look inside yourself, you allow yourself to feel the feelings that were triggered and understand where they had come from, you may even take responsibility for them – you have just done something really great! You have turned an upsetting incident into an opportunity for healing.

I used to be afraid that someone was going to leave me. I could outline every detail why my lover would meet another woman that was smarter and prettier than me, had a more fascinating job, came from a more affluent or sophisticated family, the list went on and on. I found all the reasons why I was 100% justified to be insecure, and I walked my way right out of the relationship. I was so afraid to be abandoned that I practically smothered the person I was with. This was a problem! After doing some deep work with myself I found that every inadequacy, every insufficiency or fault I had found in myself was absolutely untrue. I was perfectly fine. But I was creating turmoil that wreaked havoc in my relationships because this is what I knew; this was my adrenalin. And so I chased my relationship right out the door. Nobody was leaving in the first place. But the chatter in the mind is powerful and will chase your lover away if you don't stay present to the present, if you don't stay alert.

When you are upset and feel unworthy and undeserving, ask yourself, is it really so? Am I really unworthy and undeserving? Am I stupid, like I have been told I am, or has someone else been projecting onto me? How many of my beliefs are actually my own? How many are my parents' or my teachers' or have come from the culture at large? How have I been infected with the Story Book Syndrome?

I had to learn to change my false belief that no one would want me. I had to learn to parent myself and tell myself that I was not just "good enough" – I was great! "I am great" became my matra.

Find a mantra that empowers you, and when in doubt, when you forget who you are, repeat it to yourself. A mantra is a series of words or syllables with a positive meaning or energy that can calm and empower the mind. Hold on tight to it until you remember who you are, until you realize that you are the perfect you!

What is My Behavior Trying to Show Me?

Since negative behaviors are a symptom to a larger, deeper problem, behaviors such as overeating, gambling or promiscuity can become our gates into the healing process. Promiscuity for example, can be interpreted as playing out a desperate need for love rooted in childhood abandonment, or it can indicate lack of self-confidence rooted in childhood sexual abuse. No matter the case, it is a cry for healing.

What we learn in a traumatic childhood becomes our identity, until we unlearn it – until we heal it. What we learned, we can unlearn.

Which of your behaviors is an indication, a symptom, of your bigger problem? What in you is crying to be healed? You can turn your challenges into opportunities for restoration and growth. You can choose to do so and move forward, or you can remain where you are and play out your unresolved issues, again and again. No one can make this choice for you. This is your journey to travel. Find and release what is stopping you from building a long, loving relationship. You will feel happy and thankful – and those feelings will be real!

Life often brings us into situations that force us to go beyond our perceived limitations. To be in a healthy relationship we must be in healthy relationship with ourselves. We all have a curriculum to learn – for some the lessons are more difficult that for others. It all starts in childhood. Being abused as a child does not mean that you are damaged. It means that you were summoned to live through an extremely difficult childhood, and now, as an adult, you can learn from that experience and grow. Examine the kind of person your childhood experience has made you into. Has it made you angry and cynical, or have you turned compassionate and eager to help others?

Living on planet Earth can be seen as a training camp: our souls came into this life with the purpose of becoming more whole. In the process of dealing with our obstacles and antagonists, we can learn unconditional-love, honesty, forgiveness, compassion and happiness – and so, become more whole.

You do not need anyone in order to be whole – you are whole!

CASE STUDY

A young man came into my office and was very distraught. He had just returned from a business trip where against his better judgment he had visited a massage parlor, and let us just say, had stepped out of his committed relationship to his wife. Earlier that week he had discovered his wife's photo on a website that promoted prostitution. When he confronted her, she explained that she had overdue credit card loans she had to make payments on. He told her that she should have come to him for help, but she said that she did not want to bother him or anyone else for money. The husband was furious. The wife admitted that she had gotten the idea from a TV program that showed interviews with college students who were racking in the cash as call girls. The wife felt ashamed and guilty for needing the help in the first place, and for succumbing to the choice of prostitution.

Hearing this man's story, I asked my standard question: "Tell me about your childhood." I learned that he grew up with divorced parents. The mother was free and easy but the father was strict and demanded perfection. Being perfect included getting top grades in school. If he got A-pluses he was rewarded and loved. Perfection was the key to happiness. The need for approval and love became the motivating force in my client's drive for success.

I explained to my client that his father loved him and was doing what he thought was best. I do not agree with this style of parenting, but I helped my client see that his father had been "playing out" what he had learned as a child. The father was projecting his fear of failure and of poverty onto his son. Growing up with such a father, my client learned to expect perfection from himself and everyone else. If things were not perfect, ruthless criticism and loathing of self and others followed. My client could not accept his wife's desperate act of choosing prostitution to pay back credit card loans. She no longer fit into the box he had learned in childhood to associate with perfection. In his eyes she was dead wrong.

I asked him why had his wife been afraid to come to him for help in the first place. Prostitution may not be the most honorable way to make a living but do we have the right to judge others? I pointed out to him that he was not "perfect" when he had received more than a massage at the massage parlor abroad. He smiled and agreed that doing something that was not "perfect" without the worry of being judged had felt great. I told him: "You judged your wife so harshly, do you understand why you did it? Can you simply forgive her and yourself over this whole chain of events?"

The client took a big breath and felt relieved. Suddenly everything made sense and for the first time he forgave his father. He realized that his father's strict and demanding behavior toward him came out of love; he wanted the best for his son. His father was behaving the way he had been taught. My client understood that his wife had chosen prostitution over asking him for financial help because she was afraid of his "pointed judgmental finger." He understood that his massage parlor experience was a form of escape and retaliation – a form of playing out. My client vowed to learn to be less critical and judgmental. He understood that perfection is impossible. He embraced his new peaceful heart.

RECAP

If we find ourselves behaving in ways that are disturbing to us or to our surroundings, we better listen carefully. This behavior is an indication that something is wrong on a deeper level. We are unconsciously playing out our unresolved childhood traumas and wounds. Identifying our destructive behaviors, understanding and healing their root causes, will lead us on our journey toward the life we so wish for.

MEDITATION

Close your eyes and imagine your favorite color.... This color travels over your head, your eyes, face and mouth. Feel it travel through your shoulders, arms, heart and legs, notice that you feel very calm ... Take a deep cleansing breath ... Notice how every time you slow down your breath, you automatically relax. Taking in long deep breaths allows you to hit the "pause button."

You are lying on a wonderful blanket in a beautiful meadow ... You notice some old stately trees swaying in the breeze ... Birds are serenading you from their strong firm branches. As you look up you see the beautiful blue sky with white fluffy clouds passing by.... The clouds drift and float ... float and drift, soundlessly, quietly and gracefully, above you ... Go ahead and place your fear, your "playing out," any emotion, memory or thought you struggle with onto a cloud ... Watch your thoughts float on by.... Your thoughts are only illusions made up of your negative chatter you no longer are holding onto ... Whatever you learned can be unlearned.... Relax, be calm, and accept the lesson your illusion is trying to teach you ... allow the cloud to just drift by... Nothing you are attaching yourself to is real ... If you notice that something upsets you, understand that you are "attached" to that something and you need to let it go ... The stronger the attachment, the stronger the illusion ... so let go ... As you calmly watch the clouds float by you notice how wonderful, whimsical, they can be ... You appreciate their color, form, and the lesson they offer you ... they are your teachers ... Notice their beauty and become present to their teachings ... Think nothing, just relax, be present and breathe ... You are the sky, and the clouds are only the illusions that you are learning to bless, accept and let go of ... Breathe in ... appreciate ... and smile in gratitude.

THE WISDOM TRIANGLE

These are three areas for contemplation. You can write your thoughts, feelings, and responses on these pages or in your journal, or keep the contemplations in your mind and heart as you go about your day and before going to sleep. Your responses may change from day to day, and that is fine. Be flexible, creative, courageous – and dare!

1. What dominant behavior, or habit, in your life would you like to change?

....

....

....

....

2. What is the root cause of that behavior or habit?

....

....

....

....

3. How would your life be if you were not playing out your old subconscious programming?

....

....

....

....

CHAPTER SEVEN
PATH FOUR: ACCEPTANCE

Accepting That We Have a Problem is the
Most Important Step Toward Positive Transformation

I t is the most important step and the hardest one. *The Hero's Journey*, Joseph Campbell's mythic journey of transformation illustrated in his book *The Hero with a Thousand Faces*, suggests that after the hero receives and denies the "Call to Action," he will try to settle for the life that he knows, and inadvertently play out patterns and behaviors engrained in his subconscious mind since childhood. Eventually the hero will find himself in the "Belly of the Whale" – a most difficult ordeal that will force him to consolidate all of his powers before things are going to get really bad! In Joseph's Campbell's model, the hero is "swallowed by the whale" in the midpoint of the journey. This point is also known as "the nadir" – the point in the celestial sphere directly opposite the zenith – and is the worst and lowest point in one's state of affairs.

In 7 *Paths to Healing Your Relationship* this crisis point is ACCEP-TANCE – the 4th path – found also at the midpoint of the transformational journey. Acceptance is the hardest to come to terms with. You ask yourself: how can I accept such a devastating breakup of a relationship, or the death of a loved one, or the loss of oneself to addiction or despair or bankruptcy? And how can I accept myself as I am? Too fat, or not educated enough, or not successful enough, drinking and smoking and generally in bad health? The list of unacceptable personal traits and unfortunate life situations is endless. Well, acceptance is indeed tough and frightening, but without it there is no movement forward. Having gone through the stages of Denial, Settling and Playing Out, the rubber has met the road. The circumstances are hopeless and must be acknowledged and accepted as such.

What Happens When We Don't Accept?

We lose energy! We get stuck. Our psyche and mind are busy resisting what is happening, our perception of possibilities is dimmed, and even if the "whale" will open its mouth we will miss it and remain stuck in the whale's dark belly. Fighting against our reality, not accepting WHAT IS, is like going to ski in the winter in a bathing suit. Or like shouting to the wind when we cannot find a parking spot, as if by shouting a parking space will open. Our lack of acceptance of *what is* creates stress that can lead to serious illnesses. Medical research is now clear about this connection. When we refuse to accept ourselves and our lives unconditionally, including our problems and challenges, we are in danger of losing our self-esteem too. We begin to withdraw, and we cave under the duress of non-acceptance that swallows up our joy, creativity and talents. Not accepting ourselves and our lives fully might lead to being not-accepted by our friends and families and coworkers as well, since our outer reality reflects our inner reality. This is why you would find a severely overweight woman married to a gorgeous looking man – she has self-esteem and self-acceptance regardless of her weight. Or the opposite: a gorgeous looking man, or woman, always alone, unable to find a mate, because they lack self-acceptance and self-esteem.

If you wish to change and find peace in your life, the smartest thing to do is accept that some decisions must be made.

Why is Acceptance the Most Important Step to Recovery?

Once we accept our situation, the stuck, lost energy is released to our disposal. We can breathe now. It is said, "The truth shall set you free" ... but what now? Before we can make any decisions about the future, we must learn to sit in the discomfort of our feelings without numbing or distracting ourselves. We must feel all the pain that we have so far denied, settled for, and played out. Time to air out the dirty laundry! Time to talk about our depression, cry about our miserable childhood, mourn our dramatic love affairs, and beat the pillow about all the unfairness in our lives and in the world.

When we finally recognize and accept that we are in the "belly of the whale," there is nothing else to do but feel the pain and accept our entire life story – as is – with its agony – and its glory – and ourselves as the heroes and heroines on a journey of transformation.

Acceptance does not mean that we agree with or submit ourselves to an abusive or painful relationship; it means that we recognize what is going on, find a safe space to express our hurt, and then, mindfully and sensibly, deal with and heal the situation.

How Being Present and Acceptance Work Together?

When we are truly in the "Belly of the Whale," we are forced to admit it. There is no other way. Then and only then, the past will be just that – the past. We can no longer afford to live in the box of "stuck thinking," remaining entrenched in our past beliefs that spill out into our current lives destroying our relationships. For those who have suffered childhood trauma, or any traumatic experience at any age, accepting the unacceptable is where resistance reaches its full peak. But the only way out is through; there are no shortcuts. We must feel our feelings. It is key to learn to acknowledge and express the parts of you that hurt and then learn to soothe these hurt parts. Once we have felt and expressed our outrage and heartache in a safe way, to ourselves or in professional counseling or in any space that offers an opportunity to do so safely, it will be possible to step back and claim one's inner strength. A more peaceful life will naturally follow. Daring to feel and then comfort yourself will allow you to conquer what had gotten you into the "Belly of the Whale" in the first place.

It is crucial to remember that every unbearable, upsetting, shameful situation can be seen as a tragedy, or as a lesson to tackle, heal, and evolve. It is your choice.

When you finally accept that your life is far from being what you wish it were and what you feel it could be, it is time to find out what YOU are doing that is affecting YOU. Remember, again, that your outer world is a reflection of your inner world.

You have unintentionally created the situation you are in, and you are the only one who can untangle it and restore yourself. Running and looking the other way, pointing the finger outward, will deprive you of a possible breakthrough. It will only further distance you from addressing and tending to the part in you that is so deeply wounded. Life is too precious, why live a mediocre existence?

Work through your trauma and open up to the amazing things that will come into your life! There will still be ups and downs, but you are now equipped to sail safely through the high and low tides. You'll be surprised to realize that critical and agonizing issues will no longer take as much time to resolve as they have taken in the past. You can now identify your triggers, and rather than react unconsciously, illogically and violently, you know better: you know to stop, take a breath, look at the situation, examine your own behaviors and belief systems, accept the whole scenario, and act pro-actively – change your thoughts – change your attitude.

How Do We Change Our Thoughts?

So we have an irrational thought like "Unless I change, I will never have another lover," or "I'll lose all my money," or "my girlfriend is going to leave me"... so what do I do? Well, don't suppress the thought, but don't engage in dialogue or negotiation with it either. What you can do is acknowledge the thought, feel the hurt it produces in you, make peace with it, then use your finger and press DELETE! A space has just opened. If you don't place a healthy thought in this empty space, you risk letting another old, irrational thought slip right in – as the mind is tricky and fickle.

So settle into the empty space, relax, breathe, and change the thought: "Just because my mind is telling me this, does not mean that it is so. I am perfect the way I am, and I am sure a lover is around the corner." Since the mind works in cycles and has the tendency to repeat itself, when the same thought will emerge again, and likely it will emerge again, you will repeat the process of acknowledging, feeling, making peace, deleting and replacing. The more you practice changing your thoughts on a regular basis, the easier and faster the process will become. Since we are living in a particularly difficult time in history, life will continue to present us with challenges and struggles, but we will know how to deal with them intelligently, and with love and compassion for ourselves and for others.

Anthony de Mello, Indian Jesuit priest and spiritual teacher tells us: *"I was neurotic for years. I was anxious and depressed and selfish. Everyone kept telling me to change. I resented them and I agreed with them, and I wanted to change, but simply couldn't, no mater how hard I tried. Then one day someone said to me, Don't change. I love you as you are. Those words were music to my ears: Don't change, Don't change, Don't change... I love you as you are. I relaxed. I came alive. And suddenly I changed!"* – This is the power of acceptance.

The Turning Point

Acceptance is the turning point. The turning point means, first and foremost, turning inward. Turning inward does not mean turning away from the world or going into a cave. It means turning inward to "Know Thyself" as Socrates has taught us. We begin to know ourselves by accepting what we have denied and settled for, and what we have played out. We take inventory of our lives and begin to understand how each chapter has led to the next. We face the fact that we have bottomed out and must do something about it if we want to be happy. Isn't the mere act of admitting and accepting already a change, a turning point? When we understand our life's story, some of which has been hidden in the subconscious mind, we become acquainted with more of our strengths, and talents too. This is how we turn toward ourselves! We learn to better love ourselves, pay attention to our needs, and find healthy ways to fulfill them. Turning inward will change your relationship with yourself, and in response your relationships in the outside world will change as well.

In each moment, with every unpleasant or irrational thought, we have a choice – a turning point – to go tumbling down with our thinking, or to change it and see our state of mind and life change as well.

The turning point is a point in time as much as it is a process. It happens once, and then it happens again and again. It's an exciting journey of adventure and discovery that requires daily mindful maintenance. The payoff is huge!

It Matters What You Think, Not What "They" Think

If something in your relationship is upsetting you, look carefully into your own mirror. That mirror, your relationship, is trying to teach you what you are suffering from. What is really upsetting you? Take your index finger and point it towards yourself, yes, yourself, not them! I am upset because "I." Not because of "them." That's the key to healing. Maybe your partner is playing out a behavior similar to yours, but you don't "own" this behavior yet so it appears in the outside world, and it bugs you! It's a projection. It's a common phenomenon that someone who drinks a lot will be critical of someone else's drinking, for example. Or an over-spender will find fault and even lash at someone else for the very same behavior. This is the way in an unconscious world. This is the way of pointing the finger outward, which may take the heat off you, but perpetuates the vicious cycle of pain and blame. As my mother used to tell me and still does:

People who live in glass houses shouldn't throw stones.

For there is another way: each time we are triggered is an opportunity to look at ourselves and inquire within why are we so upset. If the answer is steeped in honesty, so is the potential for recovery and growth.

What Have You Learned?

Look back at your childhood carefully and ask yourself what have you learned. How did your parents interact with each other? How did your family, friends, teachers and neighbors relate to one another? Were they kind, warm and compassionate, offering a listening ear to the needy, or were they emotionally stingy, rigid, cold, competitive and short tempered? Who were your main caretakers and what did they teach you was right and wrong? Look back at the culture, religion and nation in which you grew up. What did these have to teach you about good and bad, the sacred and the sinful? Which ideas, beliefs and traditional values have you adopted without question, and which ones have you examined and questioned or created out of your own inspiration?

Learn to distinguish between the worldviews and values you were indoctrinated into and obligated to live by, and your own discoveries, insights and personal choices. Practice being true to yourself!

Taking Back Your Power

What would it feel like to sit in your big comfortable chair and in your mind's eye let the object of your love come to you? This can be a person you are in a relationship with, or someone you have never met but embark on the clouds of your imagination letting this person come to you. Some are so afraid to be alone that they neurotically chase one relationship after another, only to be surprised and devastated when they realize that they have just chased their lover away. Having lost their self-esteem they no longer trust that anyone will come to them so they have to chase. Others feel shame for being single and they too chase one relationship after another, or give up all together on finding love. This ways of thinking perpetuate the endless cycle of heartache and reinstalls, again and again, the illusion of unworthiness. STOP! No matter what your past was like you are worthy and deserving. When you regain, accept and embrace your genuine power, when you no longer rely on anyone else to make you feel happy, validated and whole, then life will present you with a mate.

The Practice of Acceptance

Try to have the understanding that whatever is happening in your relationship right here and now is perfect. Even when it is imperfect, it is perfect. You are who you are and your life is what it is. That does not mean that wanting to change is wrong, it just means that right now you are accepting yourself and your life as they are, and this is the most important step toward self-love, self- respect, healing and transformation. So dare to discard all that you have been taught from the moment you were born until now that no longer serves you, and accept the present moment without judgment. Choose to change the way you think, first and foremost about yourself, and let go of all the "dos" and the "don'ts" that were planted and imprinted into you.

Find the courage to rise above preconceived notions and ideas of what you should be. Become present and look at life through a new set of eyes. There is no need to dwell on the past once you have understood, cleared and healed it. There is no need to speculate about the future; often what is in store for us is way better than our wildest imaginations. Treasure the journey – be in the NOW – it will change your life and create a great future.

You are a soul having a human experience. Often the experience can be difficult. It should not be judged as wrong. Opting to see that this is true, you begin to view life differently. You understand that taking a human birth is like entering a school, and you are willing to participate fully and learn all the lessons. You recognize your gifts of compassion and insight and you generously share them with the one you love. Your past experiences make you stronger. You are able to appreciate the good in the world and contribute to it. Instead of living your life as a half-empty-glass, trust that your glass is overflowing with goodness and wisdom. No one is better than anyone else; we are just different, with different crosses to bear.

Taking back your power means that you are no longer a victim, and you don't behave unconsciously and reactively. Instead, you are mindful and live in the awareness that your relationships are mirrors that reflect back to you who you are: what inside you is gracious and light, and what you still need to accept and to heal. So give thanks to the mirror, and in so doing you will also be giving thanks to yourself.

CASE STUDY

In her childhood, one of my clients lived in a household with many brothers and sisters and their highly dysfunctional and abusive parents. As is common in such circumstances, one of the only ways a child can survive in a chaotic, unstable family is by finding some control in her own life. My client's drawers were always neat, her room in order, her school notebooks and penmanship in perfect, beautiful shape. She was always well dressed and made up, and when she was upset she never, ever told anyone and just stuffed it all in. As an adult, my client became a high power executive in a top of the line firm. But her control issues spilled into her job to the point that she almost got fired, her friends and coworkers questioned her ability to communicate, and all her relationships failed. Her addiction to being in control was ingrained in all aspects of her life; everything had to be her way or the highway! And it was "the highway." She found herself depressed, miserable and alone. This high power executive, enviable by many, spent years trying to find out what was wrong with her and wanted so badly to improve her life. During our time together a member of her family became ill. Even though my client was the one who had paid the hospital bills, she suffered abuse from her siblings. As a child, my client did not know how to deal with her parents' abuse and dysfunction. Now, as an adult – working on herself with spiritual coaching and hypnotherapy – she was able to see what was in front of her: her siblings were playing out their own hellish childhood, which they too had survived by becoming controlling, just like her. Initially she turned away, unable to deal with it, but she soon saw herself in the mirror and was able to stand up to her siblings and say: NO MORE!

My client worked rigorously until she was able to accept herself and her miserable life *as it was*. This allowed her to release her control issues, let go of the past, and find renewed strength and self-confidence. My client is dating, and her job is stronger and safer than ever – she recently got a healthy raise in her salary. What she does on a daily basis is make peace with her thoughts. When bad and fearful thoughts arise, she clears and replaces them with healthy ones. Her life has been restored. She is happy.

RECAP

Accepting that we have a problem is the most important and most difficult step on the healing journey. It is almost impossible to accept such challenging situations as bankruptcy or one's teenage child's addiction to a heavy drug, or the infidelity of a spouse. It is equally difficult to accept our own inner "enemies" such as envy, rage or self-loathing. But when we find ourselves swallowed into the "Belly of the Whale" by any such ordeals, there is no other way but to accept our reality and continue our restoration without losing energy on resentment and debate.

Inspirational Story

DR. VIKTOR FRANKL

Accepting the Unacceptable;
Finding Meaning in the Depth of Suffering

Coming upon the story of Dr. Viktor Frankl – a story that takes place in one of the most unacceptable events in human history – in the chapter on acceptance, may seem like an awkward choice. But maybe it is the perfect choice. If Dr. Frankl could have survived the Nazi death camps without losing his soul, we certainly have something to learn from his works. Reading Dr. Frankl's book *Man's Search for Meaning* has inspired and changed my life. I always pondered why there was so much suffering in the world, and while the book does not address or explain that, it taught me that in life a positive attitude is everything.

Dr. Frankl was an Austrian psychiatrist who during WWII was imprisoned for three years in Nazi concentration and death camps.

His parents, wife, and brother were murdered in the camps. It's not that Dr. Frankl "accepted" the genocide around him – of course not! But as a psychiatrist, he observed the inmates and asked himself what was the meaning behind such an experience, and what would make an inmate in a Nazi concentration camp survive such an ordeal. He writes about his insight:

"Everything can be taken from a man but one thing: the last of the human freedoms – to choose one's attitude in any given set of circumstances, to choose one's own way." And *"When we are no longer able to change a situation – we are challenged to change ourselves."*

As he was marched with the other inmates in the deep snow of a Polish winter, bare foot with only a shirt on their backs, Dr. Frankl remembered his deceased wife whom he loved very much. In that inhumane situation, as man was stripped of any dignity or respect, beaten and denigrated by the Nazi soldiers, Dr. Frankl had an insight, an epiphany. He writes:

".... Then I grasped the meaning of the greatest secret that human poetry and human thought and belief have to impart: the salvation of Man is through love and in love. I understood how a man who has nothing left in this world still may know bliss, be it only for a brief moment, in the contemplation of his beloved."

Viktor Frankl's contribution to human psychology and development is the knowledge he gained through personal experience, that in any situation, *any situation (!)* we have a choice, the choice is in us, and the choice is love. Love is another word for meaning. Love of a human, love of a bird on a wire, or for a book one has begun to write. The source of healing, tells us Dr. Frankl, is to find something meaningful to live for – something to love deeply. This sense of meaning enables us to overcome painful experiences, and can be found even in the midst of the most absurd, painful, and dehumanizing situations.

MEDITATION

Find a safe and comfortable space to sit in... Close your eyes and allow any memory, thought or feeling to surface... like oil on water. It may be a wonderful thought, a joyful memory or feeling, or a painful one... whatever it is, accept it ... let it be ... don't suppress it, don't dialogue with it ... just let it be ... in your inner space ... where it is safe... If it is a painful memory or fearful thought, don't try to stop it ... Instead, let it run wild, in your mind, the way a horse would run wild in a field. Breathe into it ... breathe in deep and breathe out long ... At some point the horse will get tired of running and rest ... Same with your painful thoughts ... let them run wild in your mind ... in your heart ... in your inner space ... like a horse ... At some point the thoughts will exhaust themselves and they will stop. Your mind will become peaceful. Underneath the pain ... underneath any negative feeling, peace resides ... You will find that peace ... joy ... love ... relief ... calmness ... even if for only a little while. Let it lift your spirit ... let it accompany you in the days to come...

THE WISDOM TRIANGLE

These are three areas for contemplation. You can write your thoughts, feelings, and responses on these pages or in your journal, or keep the contemplation in your mind as you go about your day and before you go to sleep. Your responses may change from day to day, and that is fine. So keep flexible, creative, courageous – and dare!

1. What is the most difficult thing in your life for you to accept?

....

....

....

....

2. Why is it so?

....

....

....

....

3. How would your life change if you were to accept that change is needed?

....

....

....

....

CHAPTER EIGHT

PATH FIVE: INTENTION

"The Breeze of Grace Is Always Blowing;
Set Your Sail to Catch That Breeze."

– Ramakrishna Paramahansa

"Intention" is one of the most powerful words in the universe! But not if it stays in the realm of words! It is a decision in the mind that must be followed by specific steps, deeds and actions, and cloaked in faith, if it is to be realized. Like in sailing. While it is true that the breeze of grace is always blowing – no wind will be favorable if we don't know which port we are sailing to. The Merriam Webster dictionary defines intention as "the thing that you plan to do or achieve; an aim or purpose." I especially love the word "purpose." My own purpose is to help people heal from the trauma in their lives. That is my intention.

The Power of Intention

So far on *The 7-Paths to Healing your Relationship* you became aware of denying the problems in your life; you recognized and understood why you have been settling for less than you deserve in your relationships and other areas, and you saw clearly how childhood trauma had imprinted negative thought patterns in your subconscious mind that are still playing out in your relationships, creating havoc and pain. In Acceptance – the 4th path – you learned how to let go of self-invalidating thoughts and replace them with empowering ones, and you acknowledged the necessity to change. Will all this change your life and bring you what you want? Maybe. But most likely you will need to do a little more work, and this work is using the power of intention to achieve your goals and fulfill your dreams.

The most essential intention you can make, and one that will enliven and empower every step you take, is the intention to love yourself and your life, always, whether the intentions you'll be setting materialize or not. This is a good beginning; this is setting out to sail on a clear, sunny day. Now, I know that this might not be always possible; there will be days that are cloudier than others, days you lose your hope or your faith, but try your best.

For me, when I make an intention, I declare it to the universe and ask for the assistance of Spirit. I also declare it to my husband or a trusted friend, and this keeps me accountable. In so doing, I ask for the alignment of heaven and earth to see me through. Then, no matter what happens, I accept what comes my way. I may make a course correction, I may alter the route, but I will persevere toward the goal. It is also okay to change the intention all together. For example, if you start to read a book with the intention to finish it (isn't that usually the case?) and you don't like the book, it's okay to put it down and not finish it. Accept the fact that the book is not to your liking, that there is nothing wrong with not finishing it, and declare your intention as, "Mission accomplished."

An intention does not have to be set in stone. It is not a commitment. It can be altered or terminated.

In all areas of life, from career change, to healing relationships, to eating healthy, to being kind and compassionate, an intention is needed to set a pathway toward the goal. Intention can start with a whisper deep inside, with an impulse, a need, or a dream in the night. It is important to create intentions that come from *your* needs, your heart, not intentions you are forced to make. Sometimes an intention is needed in reaction to an exterior factor. For instance, one loses money and makes an intention to earn more. A wife leaves a husband and he makes an intention to go into therapy, understand himself better, so he is able to have another relationship. Life forces us, throws us a curveball. It's also fine to receive someone else's advice, but make sure to give it your full consent and pass it through the sieve of your own understanding before you follow it.

When embarking on a sailing journey we may know our destination, we may know the route, but we may not know which ports we will be stopping at on the way, who we will be meeting, or where will we be mooring for the night. It is the same with making an intention. We make it as clear and as strong as possible, we get behind it, but best we stay open to the changing blows of grace. Grace may present us with better opportunities and possibilities than we had originally intended. Either way, our boat must be in good condition and equipped with sufficient gasoline, water and food, life jackets and such, to travel safely through the waters. Or like my husband's father used to say: "With sharp tools, the job is half done." What are some of our tools when embarking on the journey of realizing an intention? What will take us from intention to manifestation?

First and foremost knowing what we want and why we want it!

Many people don't know what they want or what they don't want. They don't know what makes them happy or unhappy, what they are good at or what their limitations are. Is it career or children, to be married or single, speak up honestly about an unmet need or let it go, be open or create boundaries? *On The 7-Paths to Healing your Relationship* we explore and clarify what your true needs are on all levels so you can set goals toward realizing them.

Goals, Plans & Action Steps

Start from the end, from the future, knowing how you will be feeling once your intentions have materialized. At the bottom line we all want to be happy! It's not whether you have a Mercedes or a Toyota, live in a mansion by the beach or a one-bedroom; it's not whether you are in a relationship or single. What matters is how these "things" make you feel. Many miserable people live in mansions, and you will find extremely happy people living modest lives. You might not be able to ride in a Mercedes right away, but you can imagine how it would make you feel, and you can live in the awareness and feeling *as if* you already have it. In this favorable state of mind begin to make your intentions. This way you are not pleading or begging, "Please, please, God help me," but instead you've created an emotional magnet inside yourself that will pull to you what you want and need, and even more.

When the sun of your own being shines brightly so will the rays of life engulf you in their effulgence.

Creating and following an intention is a fluid process with many possibilities, not a "one size fits all." Some people like to list their goals, arrange them by priorities, break them down to, say, a one-year plan, monthly action steps, and weekly tasks. Others will make a vision board – a collage with images that express their dream, yet others will write affirmations and place them in strategic spots where they can be easily seen. Some people draw statistics' charts and track their success or failure. There are also those who don't make any lists, or collages, or affirmations, or statistics, but they hold their intention in their hearts when driving a car, meditating or taking a shower. It's as if the intention is a seed they have planted – an acorn – and with their self-effort will grow into an oak tree. There are many ways and combinations, many routes to the "destination."

The journey from intention to manifestation is an inspired, resourceful process, not a military drill or boot camp.

A writer friend of mine shared with me about her practice of intention. One of her characteristics is to live by her word; when she says she'll do something she'll do it. The other day, while writing, she got terribly stuck. She couldn't find the next thought or sentence or word in the chapter she was working on, and the project had a deadline. The more obsessed she became with her "writing block," the more stuck she became. So she decided to go to the movies. It was a Monday at 11:00 a.m.! During the loud previews before the film her mind was suddenly flooded with ideas, where she had been previously blocked, and she quickly wrote them down on her cellphone. Back at home she copied it into the problematic chapter, which was now anything but problematic, and was ready to be delivered on time. When we hit the "being blocked syndrome" in any area of our lives, we can take the advice of St. Francis of Assisi:

"Start by doing what's necessary, then do what you can, soon you'll be doing the impossible."

It was necessary for my writer friend to stop obsessing about her writing block. That was the first step. The rest followed.

Commitment

Intention is not commitment. Intention is setting the goal, the harbor of our destination. Commitment is the promise we make to others or to ourselves to reach that destination. A business agreement, a marriage contract, enrollment in an educational program – those are commitments. "I intend to go to India this winter," "I plan to sign up for Internet dating," – those are intentions, there is no promise, no "contract," yet.

Since intention is not commitment, when setting an intention and not following it through to the end, we may not gain much but we also don't lose much. It was just an intention after all. On the other hand, making a commitment and breaking it leads to loss of energy and self confidence, and on the material plane can lead to loss of money in legal fees, late fees or lawyers' fees. Either way, making a commitment and then breaking it is a disappointment.

When making a commitment I suggest taking baby steps. Be mindful and do not bite off more than you can chew. Commit only to what you think you can achieve – and just a little bit more! Be gentle with yourself. Celebrate every little progress.

So you've set your intention, made your commitment, you have your roadmap and know your stepping-stones, but suddenly to "get there" you are required to take a detour. Take the detour, it is important to continue, you'll probably learn something unexpected that might even improve your goal. Don't beat yourself when things don't go as planned, don't give up, and don't overwork yourself lest you'll reach your destination too exhausted to enjoy what you have achieved. Have faith!

One of my client's was starting a new business. Along with his team they wrote down the intention for the new business on a large poster board in big, bold red ink. Everyone's attitude was top notch. When the goals were met, the bottle of Champaign was opened. When the team was off from reaching their next goal they were ready to give up.

This is what they did: they changed the color of the ink!

They replaced the bold red ink with a non-threatening calm, cool, blue. They made a conscious decision to extract the hot red fire from their motives, to cool down and enjoy the process, including the mistakes from which they could learn. The goals were no longer intimidating or threatening; they were just guides and benchmarks. And what happened? At the end of the day the company's intentions exceeded everyone's expectations. Here's the interesting part: two of the employees admitted that they were in the trenches of a difficult relationship. From their experience at the business, they learned that change was possible. They changed their attitude and worked on themselves. Their relationships shifted to the positive. They too replaced the red ink with blue.

Everything is related and interconnected. Often when we change one thing in one area of our lives, the road to shifting and improving other areas has just been paved.

When Obstacles Arise

Sometimes we just get too stuck. It is probably because in the past we experienced failure or shame or ridicule in the same or similar area. It is essential to stop and heal those painful memories. In fact, if in the past you had upsets and heartbreaks in areas you are now setting intentions and goals in, it is imperative that you heal those before you set new intentions. This way you start with a clean slate. For instance, if your intentions are about meeting someone and starting a relationship, you better look back at your past relationships, understand what had caused them to break, own up to your part in the breakup and heartache, and forgive your lovers and yourself. Your "boat" is now clean and ready to set out toward your destination.

Attitude and Gratitude

A good attitude will bring about much to be grateful for. My husband and I love to walk around our neighborhood. As we take our little promenade we pay special attention to the wonderful new restaurants and shops, inviting their spectators to come in and explore their offerings. We both feel so fortunate to be able to walk out of our front door and into a back yard full of excitement and treasures. One day, walking out of our neighborhood bookstore and heading home, we came to a stairway that led down to the crosswalk. An older couple, well dressed and put together were carefully navigating their way in the same direction. The husband had trouble walking and the wife was holding him, supporting him with every step, smiling and cheerful. We politely suggested that they walk down the stairs ahead of us, but the gentleman insisted that we go ahead of them, because, he explained, he was walking slower and needed more time. As the four of us walked down the stairs, my husband said, "We understand, my wife is still recovering, too." A conversation started. We learned that this man had had a stroke three and a half years ago. His entire left side had been paralyzed; the doctors' prognosis was that he would never recover or walk again. He continued, "Be careful, don't believe everything you hear, and never give up! KEEP A POSITIVE ATTITUDE!"

Against all odds, his intention was to walk again so he could fully enjoy his time with his treasured wife. They were now going to the movies. His eyes were sparkling and alive when he spoke about remaining positive and never giving up. You could hear the conviction in his voice. This man had learned the power of intention. For three and a half years he has struggled, and his movement is still restricted and slow, but he can walk ... with his wife, to see a film in the neighborhood. This man is my hero.

Sometimes we meet our teachers in places we least expect. Willing to listen to the wisdom of others is an essential step on the road to recovery. The world is full of teachers and they come in many forms: a stranger may have something to teach you, an animal may have something to teach you, you can learn from a plant, from the shape of a cloud, or the words of a song. Pay attention! Life will place people and sights and sounds on your path that will be signals on your transformational journey.

My Grandma Cook was a teacher to me and taught me about one's attitude to life. I did not always listen to her words but once they truly sank in they became my crown jewels. She said, "If you focus on all of the negative stuff you will find yourself living in a tornado of sorrow and anger. If you change your attitude and look for the good, you will notice that you and your relationship will shift and you'll experience happiness."

A component of having a good attitude toward life is the feeling and practice of gratitude. Being grateful for what is in front of you is life altering! I ask my clients to write down 100, yes, 100 things they are grateful for in their lives. Many people don't know what to be grateful for. All they see is how bad things are. They tell me, "I have nothing to write down." Gratitude is the fastest way to change your consciousness. If you are in a difficult relationship, turn your thoughts around: "I am grateful to be in this relationship, it is my mirror, when I look into it I can learn and change and grow." Sometimes we have a bad day; maybe we are disappointed by a spouse's insensitive behavior, or concerned for a loved one's health, or maybe it's a bad day because things just didn't work out in a business project. It is important, especially on such days, to find something to be grateful for. I personally start by being grateful for my daughter. I could spend all day doing this. I recite and feel, "I am grateful that I am so lucky that I get to be a mom." "I am grateful that my daughter is so kind." "I am grateful for the person she has become." Throughout my recovery from the ruptured aneurism, I stated, "I am grateful to be alive!"

Recent scientific research shows that gratitude supports a stronger immune system, higher level of positive emotions, more joy, optimism, happiness and generosity, and that those who are grateful, feel less lonely and isolated.

How to practice gratitude? Stop, look at your life and say thank you for what you already have. Much more will come in its wake.

CASE STUDY

When my client stepped into my office for the first time I knew this beautiful young woman was an angel. She came because she felt she was carrying a protective shield around her heart, she was afraid of men, and wanted to heal that. When she told me her story I had a hard time keeping a dry eye. The family was in the living room one day when my client's father came in and bashed his wife and kids on the head with an iron pipe, leaving them for dead. Luckily the mother was able to make it to the front door to get help. The father was incarcerated and remains in prison to this day.

It's incomprehensible how my client and her mother survived such a dehumanizing trauma yet remained kind and compassionate, not letting their inner light and loving hearts dim even in the face of such a horror. Her siblings went on to have their own families and become successful business professionals, and probably not dealt with their childhood pain and trauma. But my beautiful client, with the aura of an angel, had grown to never trust men, and has kept her heart shut and protected with a shield of loneliness. I asked her, "How does one survive this type of abuse?" She said, "Will." She explained how she'd always repeated in her mind: "I'm not going to end up disturbed like them." She was young, she did not know that what she had been doing was "setting an intention," but that's exactly what she did. And she committed to this intention and kept going.

Our work was to teach her how to forgive her father so she could move forward in her life. She made that her new intention. But it was not easy. The only way my client could process her father's attack was to understand it as a mental illness. Such cerebral understanding did not stop her however from suffering frequent nightmares and fear for her family's safety. Before she could forgive her father, she had to fully accept her life with the trauma and the consequences. She had to accept that her father had had his own issues that caused him to behave in that inhumane manner. It was not easy for her to make peace with such a horrifying memory, or to learn to live without the fear of being in a relationship in which she could be hurt again. It seemed impossible, but she did it. My client will never forget what her father had done to her, she will never have any communication with him, but she came to terms with the thought that this had been her father's journey, his "curriculum." She was able to let go of the pain of the past and center herself in the present. We spoke about the fact that sometimes it is not our job to understand why people do the things they do; still, we have to hold them in the hands of compassion and thank God we are not like them, and that we have survived.

My client dug dip into the lessons she had been summoned to learn through her childhood trauma. She realized that the trauma her mother had suffered in her childhood had caused her to uncon-sciously attract and marry a man who would end up attacking his wife and kids. She realized that her own childhood trauma had prepared her to better understand others and to be able to help those in need. This realization became her calling. She also learned that not all men are bad; in fact, most men would never think of doing what her father had done.

With the trauma passed on down the generations my client grew up believing she was "damaged goods," and fearing she'd be hurt again, she isolated herself. Working through her past she understood that the attack did not reflect who she was. She was just a little girl. It was not her fault. Replacing her self-sabotaging thoughts with positive ones allowed her to reclaim her self-confidence and strength. Her heart has opened. She now knows who she is: a worthy young woman, deserving of a healthy relationship with a partner who will treasure her, love her, and hold her in his hands of compassion. She is readily and actively attracting that.

My client, nor her mother, had succumbed to being victims of their traumatic experiences. The mother is retired and at peace, and keeps her experiences private. Those around her feel privileged and blessed to be in her presence. My client and I have become good friends. The stories of these two heroic women are a true inspiration in my own life.

RECAP

While the breeze of grace is always blowing, it is our job – our self-effort – to set our sails to catch that breeze. This is Intention. We may know our destination, we may know the conditions of the journey, but if we do not prepare, if we do not make all the inner and outer changes and adaptations and think-up all the steps and alliances, we'll never reach our goals, no matter how favorable the breeze of grace will be.

Inspirational Story

FINDING THE POWER WITHIN TO HEAL

At the height of my successful practice as a clinical hypnotherapist and counselor in Spiritual Psychology I fell ill with a ruptured brain aneurysm. Physical, emotional and financial devastation has crossed my path. I was totally debilitated, in an out of the hospital for severe dehydration and seizures. The doctors hoped I would heal but could not guarantee it. I struggled with the possibility that I may never be well again.

With the aneurysm located in the cerebellum, my equilibrium was off, my vision distorted, and I was dizzy and nauseous. All I could do was lay my head on the pillow and freeze. I was so disoriented I was not able to repeat in my head the syllables of a mantra I had been using for prayer and meditation, and was so weak I could not roll the prayer beads between my fingers. It took months till I could sit in a wheelchair, and a few more months till I could walk again. At first when I would try to get out of bed, I would stumble and fall and end up back in bed – sobbing.

Fallen into this situation I was forced to walk my talk, to take the advice I had been giving to my clients through the years, and find the power within me to heal. I was forced to become my own inspiration! If I had not yet fully grasped the power of intention to transform our lives, I sure was learning it now on the journey from being in uncontrollable physical pain and vulnerability to being back on my feet.

Acceptance, intention and trust in Spirit became my three-fold-way – my mantra – every day, every hour, week after week, month after month.

I was forced to accept that I had become handicapped and could only do what I was capable of doing and not an inch more. I was forced to accept my condition without fighting it or resenting it, without whining, "Oh, God, why me?" I had to gain control over my negative thinking such as "I will never be well again." Such thinking is natural and common in people who suffer so deeply and it's okay – completely okay (!) to think and feel that way – and yet, this is exactly the time and the opportunity to find power in the depth of despair, to find meaning, to find something to live for, to find the magic thread to pull me through. That was the time to set an intention that would be so strong, it would plow through all and any negativity like a snowplow through snow.

Deep in my heart, deeper than where the illness could reach, I knew I wanted to be well so I could continue to help my clients, and have a happy, healthy life with my husband and daughter. I wanted to be healthy and strong for her, like a firm tree she could lean on. I wanted to see her grow and experience life, and myself becoming a grandmother. I wanted to heal so I could finish writing the books I had begun, and I wanted to further evolve spiritually. All that was my intention – the magic thread to hold on to.

My faith and trust in Spirit brought me back to center whenever I lost hold of the magic thread. It whispered to me: Accept … Accept … Accept … Don't fight it … Breathe … Remember your loved ones … Remember your clients… Remember your intention … Be present with your feelings … Let them run through you without judging or fighting or resisting them. They'll eventually wash off you, and allow for a more peaceful state of mind to emerge. Remember Spirit. Remember that Spirit heals … Let Spirit do the work.

This voice, when I listened, was always right. Like a rainstorm that comes to an end, so the negative, sometimes dark thoughts, always cleared ... Right now I am in my 11ᵗʰ month of recovery. I am seeing clients, writing my book, planning talks and designing spiritual events. I go out on walks with my husband and we host guests on birthdays and holidays. I am getting better. Is there room for improvement? There always is.

Through this health ordeal I have become stronger, more present, more compassionate and sensitive toward others, aware of my own needs and how to fulfill them. More than that: I realized that the power we have within us is mightier than any outside force. It is these lessons, insights and authentic power I am now sharing with my clients. Time is a great teacher and it teaches us patience. It teaches us that what seems likes doomsday is often a blessing in disguise.

MEDITATION

Close your eyes and take a deep breath. Notice that with each deep breath you take you begin to relax. Every time you take in a deep breath you realize that your breath allows you to pause ... and the tornado of fearful and negative thoughts whirling around in your mind begins to subside. Stop and just breathe... be still and silent. Now... imagine that you are quietly walking in a beautiful field, ahead of you is a mountain, a very tall, mountain. Take your time and slowly and calmly walk to the bottom of the mountain. Notice that perhaps, your inner child is by your side holding your hand. The two of you are standing at the bottom of the mountain looking up ... You see the top of the mountain ... you feel its age and its wisdom.... you wonder how you will walk up to the top.... You take one step at a time ... you make your way up calmly and slowly … step by step … one footstep after another … Everything is perfectly okay … As you walk up the mountain you notice that you are on a path, and the path is leading you to the top of the mountain … You come to a boulder that you must push away… These boulders are "What disturbs your peace." You push these giant rocks away … then carefully taking your next step, you continue to walk up your mountain of wisdom … it has been there for a long time waiting for you to climb … You may encounter more boulders blocking your path but you're no longer disturbed … you simply push them away. Everything is okay … you are letting go … you watch these unwanted thoughts and experiences tumble down the mountain until you can no longer see them… it is as if they were never there. Take your time making your way up your path, move as many boulders that may be blocking your way … You are now at the top of the mountain … you made it! Nothing could stop you! You feel a wonderful sense of peace and contentment … you know that you can do whatever you want to do in life, the past is understood and no longer disturbs your peace … the boulders have disappeared. As you stand on your mountain of personal success you take in another deep breath and allow your shoulders to drop … perhaps the inner child does the same … you are both living in the higher realms of consciousness … you are free to be you. You embrace your journey … you feel renewed and confident to move forward with grace… you are a treasure …

THE WISDOM TRIANGLE

These are three areas for contemplation. You can write your thoughts, feelings, and responses on these pages, or in your journal, or keep the contemplation in your mind as you go about your day and before you go to sleep. Your responses may change from day to day, and that is fine. Keep flexible, honest, creative and courageous – and dare!

1. Recall a time you had an intention and it manifested.

....

....

....

....

2. What steps did you take? What helped you?

....

....

....

3. What is your intention now? What is your first step?

....

....

....

....

CHAPTER NINE
PATH SIX: SPIRITUALITY

*"Your Task Is Not to Seek for Love, but Merely
to Seek and Find All the Barriers Within Yourself
That You Have Built Against It."* – Rumi

"The Wound Is the Place Where the Light Enters You." – Rumi

What is the love, the light, that Rumi is speaking about? It is no other than our true nature that rises to the surface once we have cleared the "muck" that has been covering it. When we heal from our life's traumas and the harmful and toxic relationships of our past, we begin to live life out of our essence – which is – loving.

Having traveled through the five paths: Denial, Settling, Playing Out, Acceptance and Intention, you removed the barriers to love you had inside of you. The dust has settled. You can breathe more easily and your shoulders have dropped. You changed your perception about your life beyond your wildest dreams and feel happy and content. You are more comfortable sitting in uncertainty, and that is a powerful and not easy lesson to have learned. Having evolved to a higher state of consciousness you know that your world will unfold, as it should. You begin to live in the here and now – the state of mind where loving resides.

All spiritual traditions say that God is Love. The mystical schools of the east refer to it by different names: Nirvana, Samadhi, Satori, Mindfulness, The Tao. In Western traditions it's referred to as The Holly Ghost, the Great Spirit, Emotional Intelligence. In indigenous cultures we find a healing modality called *Soul Retrieval*, quite similar to hypnotherapy, in which a medicine doctor – a Shaman – leads an afflicted person in a process to retrieve and integrate the parts of his/or her soul that escaped the psyche in a moment of trauma. Often we hear women who had been raped say, "I left my body." After *Soul Retrieval* a person becomes more capable of living in the present and inhabiting one's body. The American teacher and author Ram Das wrote *Be Here Now* back in 1971, when the Human Potential Movement was still in its inception, and in this famous book he presents "being here now" as the way to heal, find peace, find God. Ekhart Tolle wrote *The Power of Now* as a spiritual guide for healing and enlightenment. Psychologically speaking, all of these are describing a state of mind in which we are no longer run unconsciously by our past, or stressed out and frightened by imagined fears of our future.

So what does it mean to "be here now," also known as to "be mindful?" What is the behavior of someone who resides in that state of mind?

Spirituality and Mindfulness

Spirituality is often misunderstood as some frilly practice for the faint of heart that will send you to a cave in India after giving up all your money to some Guru (this does happen sometimes, so it's good be discriminating). Spirituality may refer to any kind of meaningful activity that evokes and supports a peaceful, focused state of mind in which we are fully present in the here and now. Being mindful, living in the here and now, is the experience of an actress performing on stage, a mother nursing her baby, or anyone absorbed by a sunset or the playfulness of dolphins in the sea. This state is at the same time alert and relaxed, simple and exulted. Spirituality – being present, being mindful – is inherent to being human. One does not need to go to a church, a synagogue, an ashram or mosque in order to connect with that part in oneself. But in most cases, one does need to follow Rumi's suggestion – to seek and find and remove the barriers we've built against love inside ourselves. In other words, healing our unresolved issues will raise our consciousness and naturally allow our loving to emerge.

I wrote earlier about Papa, my French father in law, my x's dad, who, without any affiliation to a religious establishment, or Guru, without using the word "spirituality" in his lexicon, was my first teacher in the art of mindfulness, and my personal example for what spirituality can look like. Here is another story.

We were sitting in the garden of my in-laws, a 500-year old stone Chateau near Paris. It was the first time I had flown with my daughter to France to meet my husband's family. I was observing the pink geraniums in the hand-painted Italian pots next to me, the vibrancy and aliveness of each flower, each petal. Papa was working in the garden. His garden. I watched him. He was planting one flower at a time and contemplating where to plant the next one. I noticed the care and tenderness in each of his movements as his fingers dug deep into the soil, adding the appropriate nutrients one at a time, until at last the flowers were all happily gathered in their new home. Papa stood to admire the beauty of each flower as he slowly watered one plant at a time. Sometimes he would call me to come see the way light fell on a particular flower, or the shape of a leaf that had fallen to the ground. It was his way of sharing nature's little displays of artwork with me. Often his flowers later arrived on the dining room table and placed in a porcelain vase.

Papa was a painter. I would watch him stand in front of a blank canvas choosing which color to use in his painting with the same care and tender-heart he would chose which flower to plant in his garden and where. He was truly living in the here and now, present and content. Papa was loving and kind to his wife. The two of them stood closely together as one. He had a smile on his face when he looked at her, and brought her flowers and fresh herbs from his garden. He kissed her every time he left or returned to the house, a French thing to do with everyone, but with his wife his eyes were extra tender. He made sure she was safe and protected, locking the doors at night, and always taking the first step.

Most of us in the world are so busy working and rushing around that we miss half of our lives. We see nothing. Papa showed me what being present means. I learned to pay attention, to focus my mind and heart on what's in front of me, to be present around everyone and everything. Papa did not look at a flower and walk away. He took it in: the smell, color, shape. He "stopped and smelled the roses" as the cliché goes. When we really stop and take the time to not just look at things but to see them, to see their essence, even the simplest most mundane things in life take on an aura of unimaginable beauty.

The Soul and the Human Experience

A soul comes into this world with a purpose. Since life on this planet is a school, with a curriculum, and since suffering is innate to our world as we know it, this purpose will be met by obstacles, be it in a dysfunctional family, an abusive totalitarian regime, a war, and many other forms of offense. Such dire circumstances prevent the embodied soul from fully achieving its purpose, and cause it deep trauma. But facing, examining, and healing this trauma we begin to understand the story – the trajectory – of our life.

"We are not human beings having a spiritual experience. We are spiritual beings having a human experience." Pierre Teilhard de Chardin

Understanding the sacred dimension of our lives expressed in this profound, and maybe perplexing, idea opens the door to the possibility of forgivingness of ourselves and others. For instance, take someone who as a child was physically and emotionally abused by his/or her parents. In the process of healing those childhood memories, this child, now an adult, comes to realize that the abusive parents had behaved in the only way they knew how, since they too had been the victims of abuse, and without resolving their own issues abused their child (examples we've seen in this book so far). Say that the soul of this abused child had come into this world with a natural ability and desire to help others. This soul was kind, compassionate and empathic. Then came the family abuse that traumatized the child and put a lid on its soul's purpose. Later in life, the adult heals the memory of the abuse and clears and reframes the negative thought patterns created by it. The natural talents of this soul are now freed to flourish. The traumatized child has become the "wounded healer" and is finally fulfilling his/or her soul's purpose by helping others. Meaning has been found where earlier there was but sorrow and pain. This embodied soul has gained its sense of self-love and self-respect, and can be in a healthy relationship with a life partner. It is able to forgive its abusers; not forgetting, nor condoning or excusing them, though we've seen many cases where forgiveness has helped repair a damaged relationship. This embodied soul can be even thankful to the abusers because they had made him/or her who they are today.

It is an alchemical process: deep suffering can be transformed into love equal to the suffering, and even surpass it.

This is the story of such luminaries as Mahatma Gandhi, Martin Luther King, and Nelson Mandela. They transcended their suffering and turned their rage into positive action in service of generations to come. Martin Luther King said: *"Darkness cannot drive out darkness; only light can do that. Hate cannot drive out hate; only love can do that."* Or in the words of Rumi: *"The wound is the place where the Light enters you."*

Turning our wounds into compassion and becoming the healers and helpers of our world let us feel that we have not suffered in vain. Many artists, writers, composers have turned their suffering into art. What would our world be without a Van Gogh who suffered from mental illness, a Dostoyevsky who suffered from epilepsy, or a Beethoven who lost his hearing? Mothers who had been molested in their childhood and have healed their trauma become excellent mothers to their children. This alchemy is true on a large and small scale. As the saying goes: one person who has healed one issue in his/or her life moves the whole world a step forward. One person's healing inadvertently influences one's surrounding. Such a person is able to tackle life's circumstances with ease and grace. There is no longer the unconscious interpretation that "there is someone out there to get me..." Instead there is a feeling of living in a loving, supportive, trustworthy universe. We begin to live in this awareness and our world reflects that back to us: love, kindness, trust and joy...

The Book of Wisdom

Our stories – the glorious and the miserable ones – make up the tapestry of our lives. All stories from around the world and throughout history, as Dr. Joseph Campbell and other anthropologists and historians have showed us, depict a protagonist who sets out on a journey to achieve a goal and in the process transforms and grows, or resists the transformation and doesn't quite make it. The friction and struggle between the soul's purpose and the adversity it encounters causes us to evolve. The ultimate purpose in life is to evolve – and to evolve is to love!

So don't fret and don't fear. Embrace all your experiences for they are the chapters in your book of wisdom. Embrace yourself for you are the protagonist in your life story. Heal what you can, remove the gunk that hides your true self so you can become who you were meant to be. At the end of our lives, our book of wisdom will be our legacy. We are the ones who say "The buck stops here." No more abuse, no more destructive behavior, no more lies. By freeing ourselves from the chains of our past we free, to a great extent, our children and our descendants also.

The ordeals we face and overcome give meaning to our lives. What doesn't kill us makes us stronger, purer and more compassionate. Imagine the day you are older, sitting in your rocking chair, and all of the stories you could tell! I find this image comforting! Looking back at my life from the point of view of the future is inspiring for I see how far I have come, how far I have evolved. Every hardship tackled, every cross we bear one more step forward adds depth dimension and meaning to our book of wisdom. The decisions you make today will affect your future. So go for the gusto and dare to reach your full potential and celebrate who you are.

What Does "Meaning" Mean?

Think for a moment how frustrated you can become when you don't understand a foreign language spoken around you, or the plot twist in a film or book, or the unexpected behavior of a friend. Now remember the ah-ha – the relief – you feel when things are explained. The mind loves to understand. Not understanding, being in a quandary, may cause not only frustration but also lead to depression, addiction, anxiety and apathy. So how would one not become utterly enraged and troubled when encountering the brutality of war and genocide, violence and terminal illness, addiction and abandonment, or when losing one's fortune, fame or artistic inspiration. Perplexed at "why bad things happen to good people" amplifies the pain; suffering in vain is unbearable.

Now, life is way too complex to fully understand and grasp the answers to these big questions. Attempting to explain them we would be reducing the grandeur of life to the level of a child's game, or worse, into a black and white dogmatic equation. The mystery of life would be lost. The answers to most of it are beyond our intellectual understanding. For instance, why are we born to such and such parents, at this particular time, in this country? We really don't know. However, it is possible to *assign* meaning to facts and events in our lives that will shed light on some of our questions, and give us comfort, purpose and direction toward being who we were meant to be.

The dictionary defines MEANING as:

1. What is intended to be, or actually is, expressed or indicated. 2. The end, purpose, or significance of something.

I have worked with many clients and can testify that they feel much better when realizing that in their challenge was a lesson. It had been a difficult experience they would not want to repeat but it had not been in vain; they found meaning and significant insight as a result of it. It helped them climb the ladder of their own evolution. Had I not suffered some of life's challenging situations, I might not be able to help those in front of me now. The meaning of my experience showed me my path to walk. Choosing to seek and find healing, we walk out of the dark as we release the misbeliefs learned in childhood. Through recovery, we reclaim our soul and find a new meaningful life.

I think of the case of a woman who discovered that her husband was cheating on her with her best girlfriend. The couple had been married for twenty-five years and had four adult children. It was the kind of marriage where the wife served the husband, often discounting her own needs and talents. Initially the wife, bereft with grief, wanted to divorce the husband, but after more deliberation they decided to go into therapy first. It was discovered that the husband had been sexually abused as a child. He confessed to having cheated on his wife many times before. This personal discovery and exposure threw the husband into a debilitating nervous breakdown; he could not get out of bed and did not work for a year. But it was a breakdown to be a breakthrough. They each began to work on themselves. The husband understood that the sexual abuse he had suffered in childhood was among the causes he had been unfaithful to his wife. The wife realized that her un-supportive husband was a replica of her father, who had put down her artistic talents and dreams. She finally took a serious course of study and became a successful fashion photographer. For the first time in her life she was no longer at the "service" of her husband, and could now balance the family's needs with her own. The husband is no longer cheating on his wife and has resumed his work. He respects and loves his wife and has even learned to cook for himself when she is out on a photo shoot.

This couple found meaning behind the painful but unavoidable incident in which the husband's cheating had been discovered. They realized that what was "intended" behind this chain of events was for the husband to uncover and heal his childhood wound, and for the wife to put her foot down and dare to express her talents as an artist. They are happy together now. Their relationship has reached a deep level of respect and compassion for one another. The marriage is what it had been meant to be.

Look at your relationship – or lack of it – and ask yourself: what is the meaning behind it? What can you learn? If your relationship is in jeopardy, what is it about you and your beliefs that may be getting in the way?

In the throws of difficult times it is challenging, even impossible, to find meaning behind any of it. Afterwards the meaning may be revealed. So instead of condemning and judging your trials and tribulations, embrace them, view them and yourself and your life with kindness. When you don't waste energy fighting your experience, you will find that these hard times are the heralds of many blessings; their meaning will be enlightening and make your life blossom.

"If we never experience the chill of a dark winter, it is very unlikely that we will ever cherish the warmth of a bright summer's day. Nothing stimulates our appetite for the simple joys of life more than the starvation caused by sadness or desperation. In order to complete our amazing life journey successfully, it is vital that we turn each and every dark tear into a pearl of wisdom, and find the blessing in every curse."
— Anthon St. Maarten

Logotherapy

While Sigmund Freud argued that the basic human motivation is pleasure, and Alfred Adler argued it is power, Viktor Frankl argues it is the "will for meaning." Dr. Viktor Frankl's book *Man's Search for Meaning,* his autobiographical account of his time as an inmate in Nazi concentration and death camps, led him to develop the healing modality he named *Logotherapy.* Logos in Greek means "Meaning."

Here are some basic principles of Logotherapy:

1. Life itself has its own meaning under all circumstances, even the most difficult and miserable ones, the ones we think we will never get through.

2. Our primary motivation for living is our own will to find deep meaning in our lives.

3. Each and every one of us has the freedom to find meaning in what we do and what we experience, in how we act, and in the position and stand we take when faced with a challenging situation of unthinkable, unchangeable suffering.

"If there is meaning in life at all, then there must be meaning in suffering." ... *"When we are no longer able to change a situation, we are challenged to change ourselves."* Viktor Frankl

"Life has meaning under all circumstances." At times, life seems unbearable. Clients come to my office unable to function; relationships have triggered the most highly sensitive issues in their lives. When these clients resolve their issues, their mere suffering takes on a new meaning; it has led them to the brink of despair and forced them to deal with their issues. But the principal states that "life has meaning under *all* circumstances," and that includes the good and wonderful moments too. Like admiring the sunrise while driving our car to work in the early morning and just then the Beatles' song *Here Comes the Sun* starts playing on the radio. It brings a smile to our face – a little ah-ha! This synchronous moment, as Carl Jung called it, has meaning. Maybe it tells us we've done something good to receive it, or maybe it points to the "sunrise" and renewal in our own personal lives. It's up to us to assign it meaning.

"Our main motivation for living is our will to find meaning." As discussed earlier, not understanding why our life is full of misery or drama may lead to further depression, anxiety and apathy. When we begin to understand, even the most painful situations become more bearable. You often hear a person afflicted with an illness, say, "I just want to understand what's wrong with me." Or, "I just want to understand why she is leaving me to be with that other guy."

"We have the freedom to find meaning in what we do and what we experience, in how we act..." A person has inherited a sum of money – his family thinks he is going to invest it in real estate, but this person uses it to start a school for girls in an impoverished village in Africa. A couple headed for divorce court, have made up and are enjoying dinner and champagne overlooking the ocean. http://www.logotherapyinstitute.org/About_Logotherapy.html

Forgiveness

When practicing forgiveness it is important to forgive yourself and the other person. Forgiveness does not mean that one's worthiness is contingent upon your holly, God like "I forgive you" statement. When a spouse cheats on his/or her partner, the party cheated on needs to forgive the spouse if the relationship is to be continued and restored. This does not mean that cheating is accepted or tolerated. Boundaries must be established and honored, but we can choose to forgive our spouse for cheating, as we recognize he/ or she has issues to deal with. Imagine what the cheating spouse feels like. He/or she has been living in the dark shadow of secrecy and has been caught! Shame, fear and painful consequences are inevitable. As for the partner cheated on, he/or she must forgive oneself first, as most likely this discovery has brought up feelings of unworthiness, shame, and the loopy inner dialogue that goes, "If only I were good enough, my partner would have not cheated on me." Forgiving yourself for judging yourself as "not good enough," is the key to your healing! We must also forgive ourselves for judging our spouse's experience as wrong. Name-calling and anger, a tooth for a tooth, an eye for an eye will only create more misery and violence.

We can stand up for ourselves and honor our boundaries but we do not have the right to judge someone else's experience and behavior. The person who cheats on his/or her spouse may have come into this world to learn the lesson of faithfulness. To learn to be faithful, one may first have to be a cheater. Or, those who cheat may be doing so because they view their life as a half empty glass, and their lesson is to realize the half that is full. Whatever the motivation may be, conscious or unconscious, here is my advice: choose not to judge your partner's experience and behavior, forgive them for choosing a difficult path, and wish them well.

"Holding on to anger is like grasping a hot coal with the intent of throwing it at someone else; you are the one who gets burned." The Buddha

Now it's time for you to forgive yourself for buying into the misbelief that you are damaged goods. Don't judge yourself as broken; have compassion for yourself. What lesson has your experience taught you? I would think it's showing you that you are stronger than you thought you were, and can be loving and kind. Your curriculum has brought you into a difficult situation that is forcing you to learn the true meaning of forgiveness. So stop judging yourself. Free yourself from your own harmful thoughts, let go, and be grateful that you are willing to see things differently. Open your heart and allow your perception to change.

While holding on to the "unforgivable" burns like a hot coal in our hand, forgiveness is the feeling of relief, release, letting go, letting the past sail off into a misty distance; our breathing becomes easier and deeper, our minds are cleansed and open to pleasant possibilities. If we were all to practice more forgiveness – person to person and nation to nation – we would have less wars and less evil in the world. For this to take place we must heal, and healing is not for the faint of heart. Mahatma Gandhi said: *"The weak can never forgive. Forgiveness is the attribute of the strong."*

Forgiveness goes hand in hand with the awareness of the sacred dimension of life. The knowingness that our essential nature is loving, and that removing the barriers to this loving is the way to peace. But sometimes, even with the deepest excavations of our past to uncover the barriers to love, going back as far as our birth and our family ancestry, our problems are still not resolved, certain characteristics or flaws in our character are still an enigma, and no meaning is found in the inhumanity of war, famine and genocide. Because there is more to life than meets the eye. One way or another, whether we are believers, atheists, agnostics or seculars, when we are in trouble we call out: "Oh God!" Deep down in our psyche we know that as humans, we are also divine. In our own personal way we each have a connection to the Great Spirit, to the Unseen and Unknowable world, to life's awe inspiring Mystery. The process of hypnotherapy will often take us beyond our personal biography to other times and other lives to find answers. As is the story in the following case study.

CASE STUDY

I worked with a gentleman who wanted to understand why he was disinterested in making friends, felt numb when being around people, and often hid out from his long time wife. He was a nice, kind, compassionate man and none of his personal biography held the answer to his problem. After several hypnotherapy sessions we uncovered a past life that offered an explanation.

In this past life my client had been a warrior – the commander of warriors who killed and maimed innocent people. He described seeing blood everywhere; soldiers were killing civilians, young and old, for the sheer pleasure of it. As he was recalling this experience while in a hypnotic trance, his face contorted in disgust and he kept saying, "Needless, needless killing." He went on to say that the soldiers under his command were all savages, ragged and uneducated, living their lives as if they were cavemen.

When he came out of the trance he realized that the reason he was holding back from communication with others, avoiding connection even with his wife, was because he had no respect for people. In his mind "they" were all just a bunch of savage killers. "I was afraid I could be the next one to be killed," he realized.

My client and I spoke and I helped him see that he now lives in a new century. He recognized that his kind and compassionate heart in this lifetime was the result of that earlier lifetime in which he had commanded and witnessed so much "needless killing" and human suffering and could do nothing about it. Often soldiers who perform such crimes become emotionally disconnected in order to perform their tasks. To kill and to murder, my client had to become numb to his surroundings. He has carried that numbness, along with the sense-memory of blood and maimed bodies and the fear of being killed, into this lifetime. So no wonder he did not want to make friends and be around people in this present day. It was dangerous and upsetting to him on an unconscious, cellular level.

In the hypnotherapy session his mind was "reprogrammed" to trust that people can be good and trustworthy, that connecting and loving is possible and joyful. A few more hypnotherapy sessions cleared his fear of being killed. We went back into that past life and he made peace with the killer he had been back then. As a soldier, that was his job, his duty: to kill the enemy. His numbness in those wars had been a coping mechanism – a "shield" he no longer needed – for he was safe now. My client found a way to forgive his mates who had maimed and spilled the blood of innocent women and children, having been brainwashed, as is the case in wartime, to think of their enemies as "animals," thus deserving to be murdered. The past life regression work rehabilitated my client's soul and life. He now enjoys a more expanded social life, he can open up to his wife; their relationship has flourished.

Venturing into the spiritual dimension of life, into the transpersonal, allows us to find answers, meanings and explanations where our personal biographies have come to a screeching halt. Such insights open the door to deep healing, love, hope and forgiveness.

RECAP

Spirituality is both a point of view and a practice. It is the understanding that we come to this life with a purpose, and the purpose is to live in the Loving that is our basic nature. Everything we have experienced since childhood to the present day has created who we are today. The lessons we've learned amplify our wisdom and strength, our positive attitude, and our grateful hearts. We no longer point the finger; we no longer live in a "house of glass and throw stones." We have become more whole. Meditation, contemplation, chanting, art, walks in nature, are tools that help us sustain our wellbeing and bring us back to center when we fall off.

Inspirational Story

THE TEARS OF SHIVA

Many of you have seen the prayer beads originating in India called a Rudraksha beads mala. Rudraksha is a seed from a tree that grows in northern India. The seeds are strung on a silk or cotton cord, traditionally 108 seeds but can be less, and are rolled between one's fingers while repeating a mantra. The Rudraksha beads are believed to protect, comfort and heal, and play an important role in a spiritual's seeker's life. Here is why:

According to legend, these Rudrakshas are the tears of Shiva. When Lord Shiva sat up in the sky and looked down upon the earth at the suffering humans inflicted on each another he was so distraught, he kept looking for 1000 years, contemplating how to help humanity. The strain of keeping his eyes open for so long made his eyes shed tears that fell all the way from heaven down to earth. When the tears hit the ground they turned, one by one, into Rudraksha seeds.

In essence, with each roll of the precious seed-turned-bead between our fingers, and with each repetition of a mantra (whatever it may be), we pray for the alleviation and cessation of suffering on Earth, including our own. With each roll of the beads we continue Lord Shiva's contemplation. We roll Shiva's tears between our fingers and contribute in the attempt to help humanity – doing God's work on earth. What an honor!

MEDITATION

Close your eyes and take a long deep breath… Notice that as you relax, you sink deeply, calmly and soundly into the surface beneath you. With each and every breath you take you feel more calm and at peace. Nothing is important right now … this is your time to be still … all you have to do is breathe. Life has a rhythm, like the ocean waves… We know we can trust the ocean waves as they roll in and out … we trust the ocean's wisdom … it has maintained its rhythm for centuries and centuries. Life too has its own rhythm; we can walk down the stream and allow the current to take us where we need to go, or we can walk against the current in the opposite direction and have a fight with life. Quietly lift up your feet off the ground … breathe … float downstream, trust life's current … its wisdom will guide you to where you need to go …

THE WISDOM TRIANGLE

These are three areas for contemplation. You can write your thoughts, feelings, and responses on these pages or in your journal, or keep the contemplation in your mind as you go about your day and before you go to sleep. Your responses may change from day to day, and that is fine. So keep flexible, creative, courageous – and dare!

1. Recall a time when you found meaning in a problem or challenge in your life.

....

....

....

....

2. Recall a time when you forgave yourself or the person who had "wronged" you. How did it make you feel?

....

....

....

....

3. If you were able to see the entire picture, including your past lives, what would your life story be?

....

....

....

....

CHAPTER TEN
PATH SEVEN: THE NEW STORY

Free Yourself From the Endless Slavery of Your Old Story;
You Get to Choose Who You Wish to Become.

Having refused the "Call to Action" – the call to healing and transformation as elucidated in the Hero's Journey – and opted instead to deny, settle and play out your subconscious harmful story, you reached the 4th Path – Acceptance – where there was no other way but to recognize you had a problem. And as difficult as it was to admit it, you set out on the paths of Intention and Spirituality to confront your deepest fears and demons. You understood the forces that had caused your trauma, you uncovered where your root issues had stemmed from, and you have healed, and forgiven. Ha! What a journey it has been! It's now time to bring back the boon you have been granted – bring it back to yourself! Joseph Campbell calls this stage on the Hero's Journey, "The Return with the Boon." On the 7 *Paths to Healing your Relationship* this means the return to your authentic story, the one you were meant to live, the one where all your talents and natural gifts flourish and your dreams bloom.

You can take all that you have prayed for and learned, and harness its wisdom and energy to say a final goodbye to the old story of your life and write a new one. You can take this next step in confidence, knowing that your house is clean and organized, and your path onward is clear. You can move forward and live life fully, enjoying every sunset, reveling in the reflection of the moon on water, your child's smile, or the soft caress of your partner. Leave the past behind where it belongs. Say goodbye to what used to disturb you, and embrace all that life has to offer.

From a victim's experience of life to living in the awareness that your true essence is Loving and that you are the co-creator of your life – this is your new story – a heroic story as such!

While our house may be clean and in order, life does blow some dust in from the street, demanding we sustain our healed selves on a daily basis. It is our responsibility to do so; we've worked hard to earn it. Having left our painful past behind, we must be vigilant and mindful to stay in the present, to stay in our loving, lest the past will quietly creep back up into our lives.

Saying Goodbye to the Past for the Last Time

This 7th path is extremely important – like the last movement in a concert – the grand finale – after which may come a standing ovation and a call for an Encore.

The six previous paths have led us to find emotional balance and peace, elevate our consciousness, and see the world in brighter colors. Colors we can write our new story with: from pessimism to optimism, criticism to appreciation, judgment to gratitude, self-loathing to self-love and respect. Just like one bad apple will rot the entire batch it is in, so one good apple will spread its sweetness all around. You have become that sweet apple. Having healed your own hurts, you are conscious not to hurt others. You are conscious not to hurt yourself. Your family relationships, friendships, business and artistic and social life – all benefit from your own healing and recovery. If and when someone attempts to hurt you, you know how to relate to it and move on. You are able to quickly bring yourself back to your center. You know clearly which relationships are worthy of preserving and cultivating and which ones to let go of. You know when to stand up for yourself in a dispute or misunderstanding, and when to take responsibility and say, "I am sorry."

Living in the awareness that our essence is Loving, we love ourselves, we recognize our talents and strengths, and we live by them recognizing the same Loving and beauty in the people around us.

Writing Your New Story

While there comes a point where we can never go back to our old story, let us not take this point for-granted. We must nurture and sustain the person we have become. Healing is a life long journey, a deed we do on a daily basis, like mowing the loan, watering the plants, or like praying or meditating for those who do that. It is a process, not a one-time deal fixes all. In the chapter on the 4th path, Acceptance, you were guided on how to change your thoughts so as to heal and change your life for the better. On this 7th and final path you'll be guided to re-write your life story – "the story" you had been conditioned and came to believe was your story but never was – into The New Story – which is the real you!

Sustenance means re-writing your life story and then keeping it updated every day – not on paper, but in mind, heart and deed.

The journey on *The 7 Paths to Healing your Relationship* can be arduous and is not for the faint of heart. Re-writing our story once and for all, letting go of our entire life long package of misconceptions and behaviors, relationships and friendships that no longer support us can be very scary. Like migrating to another country with an unknown language, or to another planet all together. So be gentle with yourself. When we enter a lake, uncertain if the water is too cold, or too deep, we put one foot in, then the other, to test the water. So with re-writing your story: put one foot in after the other, do only as much as you can. At the same time, rewriting our story requires trust. My clients ask me, "What if it's too cold or too deep?" I tell them, "Imagine that you are standing on a diving board; you know that you cannot jump off with only one foot, that would be a disaster... so close your eyes and jump... TRUST the water to catch you."

To move forward, we must release the chains of the past and start with a clean slate. Your old story, that was never truly you, has set you up for pain and failure; your new story is the true, authentic you and will set you up for joy and success in all areas. To transition from one to the other is not always easy or comfortable, but is well worth it – trust it!

I will use myself to demonstrate how to rewrite your story. What you are about to read is what I did to free myself from an endless life of slavery to my childhood trauma of abandonment. I suggest you sit in a safe, quiet place, and take as long as you need. It's a 4-part process. To write the new story, first we have to identify the old one. Parts 1 and 2 are about identifying the old story, and I suggest you (safely) burn what you've written, to let the hurt of the past become ashes. Parts 3 and 4 do not burn! That will be your New Story. Allow Spirit to take it into her arms of compassion, setting you free.

THE 4-PART PROCESS TO REWRITING YOUR STORY

1. What Was the Situation or Incident? (This part #1 is to be burned)
My issue was around abandonment. It started with my mother, who in her childhood had experienced abandonment that had left in her deep marks. As an adult she unconsciously chased love to compensate for the lack of it in her earlier years, ending up in unfulfilled affairs that caused her much pain and led to suicide attempts. Even though she loved me, she was too busy and involved with her own life to take care of me. She always said that "I was her world," and it was true, but I didn't know it. In my childhood and teenage years I lived with my dad, a solution my mother had chosen over having me live with her. In those years I saw her only on holidays or vacations and had to witness and deal with her misfortunes, often being left alone as a result.

2. How Did it Affect You? (Part #2 is to be burned)
The effects were devastating. In the absence of a mother's attention and trust in her love for me, I grew up to become a woman who chased love wherever I could find it. Just like my mother had done, I was trying to get the love I had not received as a child. In my relationships with men I continued to feel as though I was not good enough, and in my obsessive need for love I chased them away, perpetuating the feelings of abandonment. I attracted men who were verbally and physically abusive to me, unconsciously recreating the drama I had absorbed into my bones around my mother as a child. From childhood to my relationships with men I always felt miserable and unlovable.

3. The New Story (Do not burn!)
None of it was true. My mother always wanted me and adored me! She just had too many problems of her own to be able to mother me properly. Feeling unwanted and unloved by her was my own

wrong perception and misinterpretation as a child whose needs were not being met. I know this now.

I have compassion and empathy for the journey my mother had been summoned to travel. The curriculum I have been summoned to partake in is also full of life lessons, which I hold onto and cherish for the rest of my life, for it all made me who I am today. These lessons prepared me to find my true calling and help others. They forced me to find the power in myself to emerge out of my dark nights of the soul and find the light again. Had I not experienced the darkness myself, I would have not been able to understand the sorrows of others and assist them in finding their way back to the light. Healing my own trauma of abandonment has prepared me to guide my clients down a healthy, fruitful path. I am grateful for what I have experienced and learned, the grief and the joy; I am grateful for my life's direction, my path, my Soul's journey. Life is good!

My mom is a wonderful, enlightened old soul who I love deeply. She is my rock, my inspiration, my guiding light. It is my mother who introduced me to spirituality. I would watch her light candles and say a prayer to ask for help in a situation. The candles were placed on a little shrine on a table next to my photograph, as that ensured her that I would be safe – a ritual she keeps to this day. Every once in a while she would take her crystals outside to bathe them in the sun, then place them back on her shrine. My mother was kind and taught me not to judge people. "We are created equal," she would tell me. "Just because someone may have more money than you or is more pretty, means nothing. We have no right to judge others. We don't know their story." I was young at the time and these little moments got lost in the tumult of my painful feelings of abandonment and separation from her, but now I look back and appreciate her teachings – my first spiritual teacher.

I think of my mother as a lighthouse that guides the ships to a safe harbor. Through thick and thin, rain or shine, the lighthouse stands rooted in the truth: "You will make it."

Some of us have to sail through stormy even treacherous seas, sometimes almost capsizing into the depths of our turbulent emotional storms of despair. Our lessons are often misunderstood and crush us like a tsunami, showing no mercy, leaving us for dead, a shipwreck lost in the night. It is here, deep in the abyss of struggle that we are reborn, and find our way back to the helm of our ship, sailing carefully to our destination guided by the beam of the lighthouse. The mother lessons I have had to learn are still my guiding light back to the land of safety. The relationship that had started out as a painful one for me has been transformed in my consciousness into a source of power, the firm ground where I find my strength again and again as I stand tall in the winds of winter. Having listened to the voice and wisdom of life itself, I understand that my mother has been my "instrument of change," and my sails are now well set for a graceful, peaceful voyage.

Look at your life as a prayer, your deeds and words the themes in the new story you are writing, and you will become what you write.

4. Letters to the Person, or Persons, who Hurt You, and/or to Yourself (Don't burn!)
Write a letter of love and forgiveness to the person or persons who hurt you the most. You can also write a letter to yourself and heal the most important relationship – the one to oneself.

Dear Mom,

Thank you Mommy for all the lessons you have taught me. You are so wise. You helped me travel up the learning line of life. You have always been my teacher. You have always told me that I would never be alone and that God/Spirit is by my side. As a child I remember you reading me two beautiful poems I shall never forget, Footprints in the Sand - by Mary Stevenson, and Desiderata - by Max Ehrmann.

As a child you loved and cherished me. You'd brush my hair and dress me up like a little princess. I know that in your eyes I was the meaning of life. I always knew that no matter what, I could come to you for help, love and wisdom. No matter what, you would always be here for me. You still are. Your own problems had nothing to do with me. As you said many times, "If my death could take all that I have done to you, I would let it." You did nothing "to" me. Life's circumstances had a plan for both of us. Our experiences have taught us how to be kind, non-judgmental and compassionate towards others. This of course includes ourselves.

I forgive myself for buying into the misbelief that I was not loved and that you did not want me. The truth is you always did, life was just challenging for you, which made things difficult.

I have learned that perceptions need questioning. By keeping an open mind and letting go of my own judgments and misbeliefs, I have healed my childhood wounds; they have been but steppingstones to make me who I have become. Thank you.

I want to tell you how much you mean to me!

I admire you and the journey you have traveled. I thank you for your wisdom and your appreciation for who I have become. I thank you for everything you have done, who you were and who you are today. Thank you for teaching me to believe in myself. And for wonderful gems of advise, like: "Those who live in glass

houses should not throw stones," and "we can run but we cannot
hide, wherever we go, there we will be."

I love you,
Rochelle

Letter to Myself

Dearest Rochelle,

*You have come such a long way. Your strength and courage have
blossomed your soul. You are no longer living your life in fear for
you have found your ancient roots. Your ancestors have always
been behind you, supporting and guiding you on your life's lessons.
Be quiet and still, listen to the whisper of their words. Your tree of
life has always sheltered you from the cold. Be grateful for your
experiences, for they have given you the wisdom to see the true
meaning of life. Such a gift the heavens have bestowed upon you!*

*Rochelle, you are not alone, you never will be. I will always be here
by your side. I will always hold your hand. As you walk down
the river of life remember to bless the currents you encounter. As
you continue to travel down your beautiful journey remember to
"swim down the stream."*

*Be as you are, love all that is around you, see what is before you, and
without judgment accept what you cannot change. As you walk, listen,
and fully embrace the wisdom that guides you through your travels.*

Rochelle, the greatest gift you can give to others is to love yourself.

With love,
Rochelle

CASE STUDY

This story illustrates the healing journey of one of my clients and what rewriting one's life story looks like. Included are excerpts from her own writing about her life, how it used to be, and how it is now.

From Dawn's journal

Loneliness was palpable in my big hazel eyes. Existing as a toddler with no mother is one of the worst tortures I have ever experienced. The physical and sexual abuse that found me years later never came close to scarring me as deeply as that loneliness. It is almost inexplicable. Unless you have experienced firsthand what it is like to be completely abandoned, I believe that the desolation could never be fully understood, regardless of your best-meaning attempts at empathy. It is impossible to convey in words, or any other form of communication, this feeling of being alone. Aloneness emanating from the suffocating loneliness.

In my limited memories from this time, there are flashes of my father. Sadly, after he removed my sister and I from my mother's care without her consent – which was illegal – we did not see him much. One weekend, after a visit with him, he just did not return us to her. In his typical narcissistic fashion, he merely used us as pawns to exact revenge on his wife for leaving him. For close to a year he hid us, moving us from family member to family member. He threatened my mother, and she was too afraid to look for us and did not know where we were for all that time. I still do not understand how my father, an officer of the law, and his family were able to conspire to keep us from our mother for close to a year.

It was during this year that I believe some of my most haunting automatic thoughts began to form. Like spiders, they laid their eggs deep within my mind, only to hatch at the worst possible moment, injecting me with their venom until I fell to my knees. Some of these thoughts I wouldn't dare to put on paper. Much like the isolating nature of the loneliness, if you have never suffered the indignity of being tormented by your own thoughts, you might well have me committed! As a brief example: whenever I am drowning in this low energy of abandonment, I am inundated by thoughts of me putting a gun in my mouth and watching as my skull shatters. The thought repeats over and over and over like a guillotine, crashing down just inches from my neck as I am shackled to the thoughts. Of course I am NOT suicidal nor do I have true suicidal ideations. However, I must remind myself that I have to reaffirm this within my own mind all the time. After that, the cycle continues with a barrage of more thoughts, a self-interrogation that may go on for HOURS. "Would I?" "Why would I ever have such a sick and selfish thought?" "I would never do that!" I don't want to be abandoned again, I am afraid."

When Dawn came to see me she struggled with the idea of abandonment. As you can see, her childhood has affected her life, fear took over her healthy thinking and she attracted exactly what she needed to heal. Abandonment! She had grown up under extremely difficult circumstances, so difficult, that as a small child she ran away from home and slept under the railway tracks. She kept trying to attract the "safe, loving, never leave me," person into her life, yet, she attracted instability, fear, hiding and chaos. It's what she knew and felt comfortable in.

We attract what we learn in childhood because we are comfortable with what we are used to, even when it's abuse, sorrow or rejection. We often see abused children in hospitals. Who do they cry out for? Their parent – the attacker! This is all they know. For that one-minute of love they will risk suffering an attack. These children often grow up feeling alone, abandoned and unworthy.

Dawn writes:

Abused *children always appear so blissful to the outside world. As if their smiles can hide the bruises and shame that is buried within them. I remember how much love I had for all of my abusers even as they told me they only did it because they loved me so much. What a twisted fallacy the human condition is. To feel both love and shame for one person, always trying to justify what a great person they are despite their weaknesses.*

Dawn's comfort in chaos, carried on from the chaos she had experienced in her twisted past where the boundaries between love and abuse had been blurred and confusing, deprived her of finding the better life she so wanted. As much as she tried, she kept unconsciously creating only more chaos. She just could not feel worthy and deserving of the life she wanted. Dawn knew that this was a vicious circle and had to be changed. She had to change her story.

Dawn and I pulled apart her past and she understood that her parents had severe issues of their own. We reframed both her past and that of her parents. She did not forget the abuse and abandonment, but she forgave them. After healing her past hurts she attracted a wonderful person into her life and she got married. For the first few years they lived a happy life but down the road issues she could not resolve came up. She wanted to have a child and her partner didn't. Once again Dawn's needs were not being met. Her past was creeping its way back into her life. She was not happy. But she did not want to be alone and chose to look the other way. The blurred boundaries between love and happiness were at play again. The relationship lasted several more years, until Dawn was able to honor her own needs and gather the courage to walk away. She could do this now with the help of the toolkit she had created in our work together, containing insights and wisdom, self-love and self-respect.

Throughout our work together I used Spiritual Psychology and hypnosis to help Dawn reframe the irrational beliefs in her subconscious mind. I helped her "library of associations" release her pain and judgments, and welcome forgiveness and letting go.

Dawn writes:

Rochelle taught me that I was constantly attracting people who could never comfort me or reach me because they were emotionally built to be just like my abusers so I could continue to relive my traumas until the spiritual light bulb came on. My soul knew the way the entire time, I just was not feeding it or I was too afraid to listen to it. Through journaling, meditation and reading a myriad of spiritual books I have found a way to forgive everyone who ever hurt me as well as ultimately forgive myself for letting them continue to hurt me. For the parts I played in hurting anyone whether consciously or unconsciously I forgave myself too. This wonderfully painful growth path has led me to a deep knowing of love that I had been missing since I was a toddler: self-love. For someone who always touted about how independent and strong I was—clearly this had been the missing link to that true independence.

After 30 some years of living in so many various forms of emotional prisons I can proudly navigate through so many varying situations with the strength to know that I love myself enough to be vulnerable—it is by far one of the bravest things I have ever done regardless of other people's reactions. Through doing my soul's work I have finally given myself a beautifully strong voice to tell myself that it will be okay because I have my back and all the love I ever needed was right inside me this whole time! Looking forward to more growth and attracting new learning experiences every day that continue to humble me and will forever make me grateful for this life that I am finally living.

Dawn's accomplishments are admirable. She is strong, loving, wise, compassionate and simply adorable! She is a good writer and she paints. She has a rich spiritual life practicing meditation and reading uplifting books. She lives in the awareness that she is a spiritual being having a human experience, and this spiritual viewpoint on life guides her down her path. She stands on her own two feet and is no longer visited by the barrage of invalidating thoughts and the agony of loneliness because she has herself, and what she believes in, which is Love. This is her new story!

RECAP

Our old story has set us up for much pain and failure. It wasn't really "our story," but we came to believe it was due to past conditioning and trauma. The new story sets us up for joy and success in all areas. It's a rewrite: from a victim's experience of life to living in the awareness that our true essence is Loving and that we are the co-creators of our lives – of our new story – a heroic story as such!

Meditative Inspirational Story
THE LITTLE SEAGULL

Sit quietly, take a deep breath; let your shoulders drop. As you read this story you may notice that a sense of freedom washes over you. After you read this story sit back and reflect on its lessons.

Once upon a time there was a little white seagull. This little seagull had a mother, father, sister and brother. Every day the little seagull would watch his family fly away into the sun-filled-sky and drifting clouds. His mother would soar through the sky like a magnificent angel gliding peacefully through the currents, untouched by life's circumstances. His sister danced like a ballerina in her pink tutu practicing her pirouettes. Even on a dark and cloudy day her gentle yet tenacious smile could light up the sky. His brother was the radical, dare devil, he dove like a dive-bomber into the sea beneath him, determined to catch a fish! Their protective father was always on the lookout, soaring above his family, to make sure that his flock was safe and free.

Perched on the cliff, the little seagull would sit in his nest admiring his family's talents. However, he felt trapped: his ankle was cemented to the ball and chain that anchored him to the fear of the vast endless sky beneath and all around him. One day the little seagull heard a shuffling sound. He looked behind him and saw an old disheveled wise bird walking towards him. This wise bird walked with a cane, he wore a pair of round spectacles; his white and brown feathers had turned to gray, and he whistled as he walked. Finally the wise one made his way to the nest. The little bird looked at him curiously and asked, "Who are you? "

Standing proud and tall, the ancient bird said, "I am the wise one." The little bird was puzzled; he wasn't sure what to make of this scenario. The wise one then asked, "Why are you sitting here in this nest? Look at your family, they are having so much fun." The little bird responded, "Well, I'm fine, I like it here." Well ... The wise man knew that something much larger was going on, in fact, he knew exactly what was going on.

"I see that your ankle is red and swollen, you look like you are in pain, why don't you remove your chain and heavy ball?" asked the wise old man. The little seagull looked down at his red swollen ankle, a tear fell upon his feathered cheek, and all he could say in his tiny chocking voice was, "I can't."

The wise one stood closer to his tender feathered child and softly said, "You could take the key next to your foot and unlock the chain that binds you to your pain, you could free yourself and allow your wounds to heal." The little seagull had a reluctant yet surprised look on his face; he had never thought about this before. He looked down into his nest and he said, "Well, wise one, that might be a good idea, my ankle really hurts, sometimes I feel like a prisoner to my own pain."

The wise one said nothing. The little seagull carefully took the key and unlocked the ball and chain. The heavy chain and ball fell to the floor and relief washed over the little seagull's face. He sighed deeply, and with a sweet peaceful smile his shoulders dropped as though the weight of the world suddenly had been lifted off his weary wings.

"Now little one, let us fly with your family in the land of freedom." The little seagull, stalling, fearfully said, "No, no, no! I am fine right here... I think I'll just watch, I have a good seat, you know." The wise one looked over his spectacles and with deep compassion asked, "My son, but why are you so afraid?" The little seagull cowered. He lowered his head and said, "Oh, I am afraid I may fall, I may plummet into the stormy seas of death!" The wise one held the little seagull gently in his old and frail feathered wings and explained:

"My son, you are a bird, you were meant to fly; this is your birthright. Look at men, their desire is to experience freedom as we do, they want to travel as we have for thousands of years. They have built airlines, hot air balloons, they even sky dive! But, my son, they will never grow feathers, they will never experience what we birds experience. You were meant to fly, your ball and chain are no longer holding you down, it is time for you to spread your wings and be the extraordinary bird you are. A beautiful, elegant, white seagull."

Well, the little seagull was paying attention. A little smile curved on his face, a look of temptation appeared in his eye. He took a long slow breath. "Wise one," the little bird told the old bird, "if I say yes, will you jump off this cliff with me?"

"Yes my son, yes," came the old bird's response.

The little seagull leaped out of his nest. Slowly and carefully he walked to the edge of the cliff, closed his eyes and said, "Okay, when I count to three we will jump into the heavens, oh, tell me I will not fall."

"No, my son, you will not fall, remember you are a bird, you were meant to fly."

The little seagull stood brave and strong, and with determination he counted, "One – two – three!"

He leapt off the cliff and into the sky. Much to his surprise he flew amongst the currents of the wind, he twisted and twirled and flew and glided like no other seagull had ever flown. He even dove into the sea and caught a fish! When he looked down at the seashore he saw his family seated on the beach and looking up at him. His father's feathers puffed in pride, his mother's eyes filled with tenderness and love, his brother and sister cheered his glorious first flight.

All of a sudden a large shadow loomed over his family sheltering them from the hot scorching sun behind him. It was he – the little bird! His little seagull's wings had spread across the sky like a thousand angels. His newly found freedom filled him with awe and joy.

As he casually glanced back at the nest he saw the wise one perched on a rock. Confused and a bit angry he flew back to the cliff, stood in front of the old wise one and sternly spoke:

"Wait a minute, you said that you were going to come with me! I jumped off the ledge all by myself, I could have fallen and plunged to my death!"

The wise one looked up through his spectacles and said: "My son, I did not need to go with you. I wanted you to learn to trust yourself, to leave your fears behind and jump. I always knew you could fly."

THE WISDOM TRIANGLE

These are three areas for contemplation. You can write your thoughts, feelings, and responses on these pages or in your journal, or keep the contemplation in your mind as you go about your day and before you go to sleep. Your responses may change from day to day, and that is fine. So keep flexible, creative and courageous – and dare!

1. What is your old story – the one you believed was the story of your life?

....

....

....

....

2. What is your new story?

....

....

....

....

3. Where is your new story leading you?

....

....

....

....

CHAPTER ELEVEN

REFLECTIONS ON PARENTING

"Each Day of Our Lives We Make Deposits in the Memory Banks of Our Children."

Charles R. Swindoll

Favorable as well as dysfunctional ancestral family patterns are transported from generation to generation. In the case of the latter, in order to stop the dysfunction from perpetuating, it must rise up in the awareness of a family member down the line who will heal it. I was unconsciously perpetuating my "mother wound" – my abandonment trauma – and risked passing it on to my daughter, until the shocking truth stared me in the face and could no longer be ignored.

In my early years of motherhood I remembered my feelings of abandonment, and was afraid that my daughter would feel left alone and unloved too. To make sure this would not happen, I compensated. Over compensated: I constantly told her how much she meant to me, how much I loved her, and I spent every moment of the day with her, often at the expense of my own needs. I was giving my daughter what I had never had – a 24/7 mother.

After the divorce, I began dating. Suddenly my child, who had been the center and focus of my attention, was no longer that. Even though I never left her alone, never a day passed by without my covering her with love and adoration, the divorce had brought up in me my unresolved childhood trauma, forcing me onto a rollercoaster ride from joy to depression, up and down, up and down, and my daughter felt the grunt of it. To soothe my pain I chased one man after another until I ended up in a relationship with a man who was extremely abusive. When I tried to leave the relationship he would find a way to threaten and pull me back in, as if I were a puppet on a string. Because of this man I lost money and my business. As much as I tried to protect my daughter from witnessing any of it, it was impossible. She saw it – she was eight years old – old enough to understand that something was deeply wrong with her mother. I was in the throws of a severe depression and had to be institutionalized. My child was affected. The thing I was trying to prevent the most I could not prevent. My biggest fear had always been that my daughter would feel afraid of losing her mother, that she would feel abandoned, and here it was: she saw me in the hospital and she was terrified.

"I don't want you to die, Mommy," she said to me, just like I had said to my mother so many years earlier when she was hospitalized after trying to commit suicide.

The seven days I was institutionalized were the final straw. The shocking truth stared me in the face: my daughter is going to end up with an abandonment trauma just like I did. This is when I said

"The buck stops here." I had to change. I had to heal the pattern of abandonment, lest I passed it on to my daughter.

Using the practices and processes described in this book, I healed myself, and have since provided my daughter with a safe and loving environment to live in. We speak frankly and we trust each other. She knows that life is far from perfect, but she also knows how great life is. We've been through a lot together and on the journey we bonded so deeply.

It is my mother who had pushed me down to the underworld of abandonment where I unconsciously chased love that brought me to my knees. It is for the sake of my daughter that I willed myself to get up on my own two feet and learn my biggest lesson – that I don't need anyone to make me whole – I am already whole. The pattern had been broken.

To support your child in having a happy healthy life, heal your own trauma, lest you risk transmitting it on. Unless your issues are made conscious and your sorrows healed, you will pass them to your descendants.

In all relationships, as illustrated in this book, a problem in our outer reality is a reflection of an imbalance or unhealed issue within us. To heal our outer world, we first must heal ourselves. Who, if not our children, are our clearest, sharpest, most accurate mirrors? They are our daily reminders to tend to our own gardens, heal our issues so we don't project our childhood traumas all over them. When we work on ourselves and take personal responsibility, we stop pointing the finger and play the blame game. This is a good role model to exhibit to our children. It should come as no surprise that parents who are mindful and work to heal their own childhood traumas will see a positive shift in their children's behavior.

Children Don't Talk

A well-known phenomenon predicates that children accept and forgive what they see in their homes; they need their parents so they accept the good with the bad. Even when they feel deep inside that something in their parents' behavior is wrong they make it right and adapt to the situation. Sometimes children are sworn to secrecy, often threatened into secrecy. Children will keep their suffering to themselves so as to protect their parents. This is why a sexually abused child will keep the abuse secret, or children of alcohol or drug-abusing parents will not disclose what's going on in their homes. There are many variations and storylines to the "children don't talk" phenomenon. One of them I saw first hand with my own child.

When my daughter was in elementary school I noticed that she had become somewhat shy and withdrawn. Before, she had been a bubbly outgoing little girl, but now she seemed quiet and keeping to herself. When she'd come home from school I would ask her, "How was school today?" She would reply, "Okay." I would continue, "What did you do?" She would reply, "Nothing," then turn away and go to her room. I thought she had had a long and tiring day at school and I did not want to interfere with her choice to be left alone.

One day, a few years later, she was in middle school now, I complimented her on how smart she was, and what a good student. She turned to me and said, "That's not what my elementary school teacher said." And she went on to confide in me that her first grade teacher had told her that she was not intelligent, and she was put in groups beneath her intelligence level.

It was a terrible thing for a mother to hear. I knew how bright my daughter was and felt bad she had been the victim of such treatment by a teacher. I understood that when she had spoken to me in monosyllables without meeting my eye, she was covering up how distraught she was feeling inside. I asked her, "Why didn't you tell me?" She said, "Children don't know the words to express their feelings. They don't understand what is going on, they just become what they feel." In my daughter's case, she withdrew into herself. I felt so mad at myself. I should have asked her more specific questions, like, "What did you study in school today?" or "What is your teacher like?" or "Do you like school?" Since then, I have been asking her many questions and we've had long talks that helped me understand her better.

I understood why she was complaining that her stomach was hurting and asked to stay home from school. When she was nervous, her stomach hurt – and school made her nervous. We discussed it. I reminded her how smart she was, I helped her feel extra safe, and she went to school and was able to belong with the rest of the children. Our conversation had eased her stomach pain. My daughter has since become incredibly strong, self-sufficient, well adjusted, and all around a magnificent person. She has a good head on her shoulders, a good heart, and both feet on the ground. I have learned from my mistakes, and am deeply grateful to be a mother. My two favorite holidays are Mother's Day and her birthday on St. Patrick's Day. Yep! She is my little lucky charm. My child is the greatest gift I will ever receive. We are very close and can talk about anything. I love her more than anything and enjoy watching her life unfold.

This is what I learned from my daughter: I learned that when children become even slightly illusive, it means that they are hiding something. Children feel, but they don't know how to describe what they feel so they react: some become angry and sad, others become shy and withdrawn. It is their subconscious cry for help, the only way they know how.

I tell my clients, "If you notice a change in behavior in your child, I recommend you seek professional help. A child psychologist is trained to see things that we parents do not always see. As parents we must never assume anything."

Take the time to play and speak with your children. Ask questions. When you play with them, watch "who" and "what" they put in their dollhouse or their toy truck. If they watch a particular TV show, speak to them about it, ask how are the people in the TV show like people in their lives, and how are they different. Is a friend in school like a good person on TV or a bad one? Watch your child's response carefully, without judgment or interpretation, listen to what they have to say. You will learn a lot about your child's life.

It's Not the Child's Job to Take Care of the Parent

In my practice I have only too often seen that children find themselves in a position where they are compelled to take care of their parents. A mother will cry on her daughter's shoulder about a neglectful husband or ex or lover; a father will release his despair about money and debt to his ten-year old kid. This is not right. Often the child will take in the problem as if it were his/or own fault. They will carry the parent's fear and shame into their adulthood, allowing it to taint their own lives. The adult is responsible for parenting the child, not the other way around!

What children hear and absorb in the home shapes their minds, their thinking, their emotional landscape. Verbal criticism like, "You're stupid," "you're a daydreamer," "you will always struggle in life," spoken to a child in the heat of an argument will lodge into the child's subconscious mind. As an adult, say under the duress of a job interview, the messages from childhood will pop up – "You're stupid" "you're a day dreamer" – robbing the person from the possibility of doing well on the job interview.

In the field of hypnotherapy we call it the "library of associations," and it is formed in childhood and located in our subconscious mind. Everything we experience, see, hear, understand or not understand goes into this library. When parents fight in front of their pre-verbal children, thinking the young child will not understand or remember it, they are wrong. It all goes into the child's subconscious mind and lodges there. A toddler hears his/or her parents quarrel: "You are a terrible mother!" ... "I could kill you now!" True, they don't understand cerebrally what they hear, but it goes into their sub-conscious with all the negative energy the parents have expressed. Now in adulthood, this person has an argument with a spouse. The messages from long ago pop out from the library of associations: "You are a terrible mother," "I could kill you!" – messages that overtake any possibility for good, civil and logical communication.

Children are little humans; treat them with respect. Understand that you, the parent, are their teacher. Your education is for life! So share your wisdom and keep them safe. Teach what you think will benefit them. Create a safe container for your children to live in. Give them the freedom to discover their own wants and needs – but keep an eye on them. Don't ever raise your hand on your kids, or threaten them, or call them names. If you find yourself doing this, please take a look in the mirror! If your child is acting out, I suggest you get help.

You Cannot Love Your Child Too Much But Don't Suffocate It With Love Either

Children need to be nurtured and cultivated like a plant or a garden or a work of art. In fact they are your highest and finest works of art! They need to be acknowledged for their talents and strengths, supported in their weaker areas, and always told how wonderful they are. If you can't do that, you probably have not healed your own emotional wounds and are most likely projecting them onto your child. For example, if you had fallen into a deep lake as a child, are you now overprotective about your children, instilling in them the fear of water and depriving them of much fun and exercise? If you had fallen off a bike as a teen, are you forbidding your daughter from riding a bike? Examine your own childhood and how your experiences and beliefs affect your parenting. You can apply the "7-steps" to the parent-child relationship. Is there pain or upset your child is denying? Is your child playing out a wounded part in her/or himself by self-medicating? Has your child witnessed something that a child should not be witnessing? You can teach the "7-steps" to your children – you will be gifting them with a precious gift! Talk to your children. Ask questions. And above all – LOVE THEM and let them know that you do!

Parental love is the foundation for being secure, self-confident and successful in adulthood.

Children deserve a chance! Help rid them of misunderstandings they may have about themselves and about life; make them aware of their negative self-talk and self-judgments, and teach them how to replace those with positive thoughts. Teach them to love and respect themselves. Teach them forgiveness, compassion, acceptance, kindness, patience and courage. If you make a mistake, be gentle with yourself and forgive yourself. You can always ask forgiveness from your child too. It is a great teaching to show a child that when making a mistake it's all right to say "I am sorry." Your children are watching your every move, be MINDFUL.

Teach your child to keep a good attitude and self-love, especially when life presents challenges and obstacles.

I recently worked with a young woman who since childhood had wanted to play the piano and sing but her family had insisted that she become a doctor, because doctors make good money. The parents had both grown up in poverty and still carried the shame of that life; they wanted to give their daughter the life they could have not had. But my client did not care about money and did not want to be a doctor; her heart was full of song, she wanted to stand on the stage and serenade the world like a little nightingale heard by all.

I worked with my client for about a year. She had a hard time reconciling her desire to play music and the feeling that she was betraying her parents. They had raised her and she felt she owed them. If she followed her heart to become a musician, her family would have abandoned her. She wanted their love and approval. After much inner work this young woman finally found the strength to dare and go after her dream. She moved to New York, enrolled in a music school, and began performing. The family is still disappointed but slowly coming to a place of acceptance. The important thing is that my talented client is doing what she loves!

I believe in respect and love for our parents, but a person is entitled to carve out one's own life. I tell parents: you've had a chance to live your life, please allow your children to live theirs. They have their own curriculum on the ladder of spiritual and psychological evolution; they will learn from their success and failure. Empower them, but don't dress them up in your own fears and flops.

Letters to Santa

When my daughter was young, one of the ways in which she expressed her feelings was to write in her pink sparkled journal. She wrote letters to Santa Clause. I believe that writing in her journal, she was speaking to the Great Sprit. When she wrote to Santa she was talking to someone she believed would help her. She trusted in magic. Once, before Christmas Eve, I secretly read one of her letters. To my surprise she did not write what things she wanted from Santa, that she had already told me. Her letter to Santa was different. She asked that all the pain and suffering be removed from her life. She wanted a happy family, no fighting, no pointing fingers, just happy. She asked for the health of her dogs, Happy and Lucky, and she wanted her mommy and daddy to re-marry. As I read her words my heart grew heavy. I wanted to help her. All I could do was ask Santa to write her back.

On Christmas morning, along with the toys she had requested, Santa had left her a letter. In it he explained to her that sometimes adults do things that little children do not understand. He wrote to her that she was loved and cherished and that she should never worry, everything would be okay. She was pleased and comforted reading Santa's affirming letter.

As for her journal, out of respect I only glanced at a few pages. I wanted to better understand my daughter's thoughts so I could help her deal with her upset around the divorce.

It is important for children to have outlets to express their feelings, both joyful and troubling. Help your children find creative ways to channel their energies.

CASE STUDY

"Boys Don't Cry" and Obsessive Perfectionism

Many clients have walked into my office expressing fear that they would be abandoned or punished for having done something wrong. This was the case of a man, born in a foreign country, and his younger sister. As a young child, this man had been left behind with his grandparents in their country of origin while his parents came to the U.S. to earn a better living. The grandparents were strict and inflexible and raised the child in the old school method that proclaimed that "boys don't cry." My client was never allowed to cry, not even after being apart from his parents for eleven years and missing them terribly. If he shed one tear he was scolded and hit by his grandparents. "Stand tall, hold your head high, and get over it," they ordered him. This was acceptable education in that country, that culture, though such rigid education can be found in all countries and cultures. "Be glad that we have a roof over our heads and that your parents are sending us money every month!" the boy was told. This poor child grew up having nowhere to turn, no one to trust, always afraid that he would be abandoned again. The first time this man came to see me his pain exploded out of his mouth: "Why? Why did they leave me? Didn't they love me?"

His sister, like many others in their culture, carried the weight of academic perfection. She spent all her days in school, sometimes seven days a week. If her report card was hexed with a horrifying B she might as well have received an F, for FAIL! This girl had no childhood. She rarely played or took part in non-academic school activities. For the rest of her life she feared failure. If something in her life was not perfect she would freeze in pain and cry. If her children or husband had a problem she felt it was her fault. She expected perfection from everyone around her. Perfection haunted her life. Once, her daughter used her mother's hairbrush without permission and afterwards did not clean it. Disaster hit as if a tornado had destroyed an entire city. The daughter was grounded for a month. The mother fell to the floor unraveling and chastising herself for her daughter's neglect. The children were forbidden to fail their classes and ended up hating school. The mantra their mother indoctrinated them with, was, "I will go to the best schools, I will be a doctor or a lawyer, I will make money."

I worked individually with both brother and sister using the *7-steps* until they each understood and accepted their particular childhood within a cultural and historical context. They came to terms with their life stories that had been shaped by the hardships of war and poverty. I explained to the brother that his parents and grandparents had done the best they could and knew how. For his parents to have stayed behind would have been even worse, and would have deprived him and his sister from eventually being brought along to live in the U.S. I invited my client to feel and express the pain he had not been allowed to express in childhood. I invited him to cry and to grieve his sad upbringing. The brother realized that his family loved him, but that their culture did not invite demonstrative deeds of love and affection. He forgave them. He put the past behind him. He learned to love himself and re-parent his inner child by reassuring it: "I am here for you, and you are here for me, we will love each other to the end of time. We will never be alone, we have each other." One year later this man was happily married.

The sister, becoming conscious of her ingrained patterns of perfectionism and control, apologized to her children. She stopped being so strict in disciplining them and allowed them to play and be the innocent little creatures they were meant to be. They no longer had to become a doctor or a lawyer. Their new mantra was changed to, "I am going to do the best I can and that is just fine." My client, the sister, quit her job as a lawyer and is now teaching pre-school. Her class is full of art projects, gardening and cooking. In this new job she can be the child she had never been able to be. She has healed herself from the perfection syndrome and has created a happy and creative household for her children.

The brother and sister are no longer haunted by the fear of abandonment and the obsession with perfection. They have found a new appreciation for the culture and tradition they came from, and empathy and respect for those who have sacrificed to offer a better life to their children in the U.S. Brother and sister have set themselves free.

It is vital and imperative for a child to be allowed to feel the entire rainbow of one's feelings.

Perfectionism is an inbuilt mechanism for failure. Doing one's best is good enough. Teach your children to avoid comparing themselves to others; such comparisons usually lead to a feeling of failure – there will always be someone out there that is better than us. But teach them to compare themselves to themselves – how they were just a little while back – and realize how far they have come. Teach them to acknowledge their own progress; this is how the road to success is paved.

RECAP

When it comes to children, we, as adults, must pay attention to our words and behaviors. Many adults suffered trauma in childhood and are now projecting it onto their children. An abused child will grow up recreating more abuse for oneself, and eventually become an abusive parent. The pattern is passed from generation to generation until someone down the line says: "The buck stops here," and heals the pattern. Our children are the future of the world and our most precious asset; to be a great parent requires healing our own wounds.

TREE: A MEDITATION

Relax and allow your shoulders to drop ... release any old story you no longer wish to hold. Imagine that you are a block of ice sitting in the sun. Drop by drop you gracefully and gently melt away until you become a cool pool of water. You no longer hold onto the frozen block of beliefs. You can flow now in your pool of water. Relax, find the calm inside yourself and float into the next story.

Imagine that you are walking in a beautiful meadow, a field full of pretty wild flowers swaying in the breeze ... it is as though they are a symphony of purity and bliss. Their trumpets alert your arrival. As you continue to walk you notice the weather ... is it hot? Is it cold? Sunny? Warm? You feel a sense of calm as mother Earth grounds you in her presence. Step by step you notice your breath quietly leading you to the most magnificent tree you have ever seen.

You stand in front of. "Tree" – you feel her wisdom and love. She is understanding, present and strong. You feel a little tired, so you sit down on her grassy carpet and lean against her ancient wrinkled trunk. As you rest upon her safety, you notice her branches are dancing to the currents of the wind, her leaves rustle as they shelter you from the elements ... the tiny bluebirds serenade you with their new delightful song.

You rest and take in all the gifts Tree has to offer you. Her undying love and affection, her protection, strength and beauty are yours to hold and lean on forever. As you take a deep breath you let out a sigh ... you feel her roots beneath you, the comfort, the triumph and pain, spread for miles and miles, as far as the eye can see. Their history and wisdom anchor you to your inner knowing, that life will be fine. At anytime you can take in a deep breath and feel the Tree's presence behind you, you can lean on the trunk for support, her arms will embrace you, her gentle voice will softly whisper, "I am here, you are here, you are where you need to be. Allow your smile to warm your heart, allow your soul to flourish, accept and honor your rainbow, the one with all the colors that lead you down your new and fruitful path ... I am here."

As you continue to take in all the beauty around you, you notice that one of the tree's branches has been damaged, burnt and torn by the lightning that had struck her in the heat of passion. The seasons they come and go, the rain, snow, the hurricanes of life attempt to destroy her beauty. But no, she says, "I am here, I am Tree." She stands in her truth, in her grace and dignity, with her wise roots deep below she'll weather any storm.

"You" she says, "you can count on me. I am your sturdy trunk to lean on. I am you – I am Tree..."

THE WISDOM TRIANGLE

These are three areas for contemplation. You can write your thoughts, feelings, and responses on the page below, or in your journal, or keep the contemplation in your mind as you go about your day and before you go to sleep. Your responses may change from day to day, and that is fine. So keep flexible, creative and courageous – and dare!

1. What did your parents project onto you?

....

....

....

....

2. What have you projected onto your own children?

....

....

....

....

3. What have you learned from your child?

....

....

....

....

CHAPTER TWELVE

CONCLUSION:
FROM GRAPES TO VINEGAR

Accept and Honor All Your Past Experiences, Good and Bad,
so You Can Flavor the Palette of Your Own Life.

The village where my mother and father in law, who I called Maman and Papa, lived in their 500-year-old stone Chateaux, was the kind of village you see in movies depicting the French countryside: villagers strolling through the square carrying wicker baskets as they shop for fresh bread and pastries or select fresh vegetables and fish in the outdoor market. The market had been central to the life of the community since its inception in the sixteenth century; a feast to the eye then and now in its colors, textures and beauty.

In France food is not just food; every meal is an event. Maman would set the table with great care, protective of the delicate china she kept in an antique armoire. She would iron the cloth napkins and place them in front of each table setting, folded just so. Once the table was set, she would go out to the organic vegetable garden that she and Papa had planted, and collect fresh herbs she would then toss into one of her salads she was so well known for. Invariably, and almost at the same moment, Papa would burst through the door proudly waving the fresh baguette he had picked up in the village market – a big smile on his face. It was Papa's job to take the cheeses out of the refrigerator and place them on a platter so by the end of the meal they'd be in perfect room temperature and ready to be consumed with fresh fruit and a digestif liquor.

Still before the meal Papa would whisper to me to follow him down to the cellar, which was spotless clean, not a spec of dust could be detected, for it was always in use. Papa would search for today's prize, and there it was right on the top shelf – a large, white ceramic container. He would very carefully open it, and POOF, the room was flooded with the scent of the pungent aroma of vinegar!

You see, after every lunch and dinner, our friends' and family's wine glasses would have a little bit of wine left in them. Papa would quietly make his rounds, tiptoeing around the table gathering up the unfinished wine and pour it into the white ceramic container. Every last little drop of it!

These collected wines would sit for many months in this one container, mixing and mingling, sharing their stories with one another, crying, laughing, and becoming one very unique blend of vinegar comprised of all their collective parts. The "m'ere du vinaigrette" would allow the wines to transform into new and delicious gourmet vinegar that Maman would drizzle on her salad, transporting it to something beyond perfection. This "m'ere," the medium that produces the vinegar, became the mother to the wines as they melded their stories; she held them in her arms with compassion and love until their lives became enriched and new. Oh, how I treasure these memories.

Just like those collected wines, our own stories, good and bad, red and white, make up the tapestries of our lives. Our souls are here to learn the lessons this time around. I tell my clients to embrace their experiences; they are the chapters in their own book of wisdom. Nothing is simply bad and you and I are not "injured goods." We belong in the circumstances we choose to be in. Being worthy and deserving are inherently who we are. We do not need to do anything to merit or prove that we are. Simply by being born, you are worthy and deserving.

What you must do is heal the past hurt so you can learn from it, and then move on. When we reach the end of our lives, our own book of wisdom will become our legacy. The wonderfully unique "vinegar" that we become is simply the ultimate outcome of all the stories and "wines" that we have tasted and blended together.

Although a grape is just a grape, through time and change it can take on many forms. All of your experiences can be harnessed to allow you to embrace an enriching relationship. Not only with others but with yourself as well! And think of all of the wisdom you will bring to the dinner table!

I am thankful for all the lessons I have learned over time. This is not to say that I would be anxious or eager to relive them, however, if I had not gone through my own personal "war of life," I would not have the experience, nor the wisdom, to help others through their "wars." It is my destiny to do this and I am humbled by the privilege.

Each of us carries a shield and a sword. Our shield protects us so we can take the next step and continue our journey. Our sword allows us to fight those inner demons, to defeat them and to scale to the top of our personal, beautiful and dangerous "Everest" mountain. By examining and living through all that you are, you will see how all the positive and negative forces have shaped you as a person. The positive memories will help you trust the light that guides you forward on your journey.

In working the 7 *Paths to Healing your Relationship* with me you will dig deep and discover the root issues that are stopping you from living the rich and healthy life that you desire and deserve. I often tell people that we get what we think of the most. You will experience and receive what you focus on. When you honestly understand the influences and experiences in your past, and you heal the painful memories, you will travel the remainder of your life joyfully embracing your new journey.

As a healing exercise, start a journal and write down daily all the good and positive things that happen to you. What are you grateful for? Soon you will see that your existing way of thinking about what is positive and negative will change. You will begin to feel better about yourself and about your life because your perception of what is good and bad would have changed. Those "not so hot" experiences will be understood differently, they'll drift away and become inconsequential. You will learn to reframe your old negative thoughts as opportunities and lessons to learn from.

Remember, if you live in the here and now, embracing all events, you will not be projecting your troubled and negative past into the future. This behavior only creates worry and despair, which in turn traumatizes your present. In the here and now be open and welcoming, generous and hospitable. Get rid of the judgments and negative chatter from your past, those old, unproductive tapes you have been playing in your head, and the here and now you seek will be yours. The here and now is all any of us has. It does take great strength and courage to change your thinking patterns; as adults we have become what we learned as children. End this, and experience the power of now.

No matter how difficult your childhood and past have been, you know them. You are familiar with them. The mind would rather hold onto outdated patterns, what it knows, rather than change into something new and unknown. This is why habits are so difficult to break – we don't want to leave the known comfort zone.

Change your patterns and your thoughts, and your life will change. Accept and honor all your past experiences, good and bad, for they are the grapes, the left over wine that comingles in your internal "m'ere du vinaigrette," so you can flavor the palette of your own life.

Rochelle L. Cook Biography

Rochelle L. Cook is a clinical hypnotherapist and consultant in spiritual psychology with a fresh and innovative approach to healing.

Rochelle utilizes effective spiritual and traditional techniques of Hypnosis and Gestalt methods to ignite "Rapid Healing."

Her background and life experiences allow her to connect to a diverse population of all ages. Her philosophy is that all people are worthy and lovable; they just haven't fully embraced that yet. Rochelle's passion is helping people get to the good and find the love inside they deserve.

Rochelle L. Cook, The Soul's Coach, is one of the most respected practitioners in Clinical Hypnotherapy and Spiritual Psychology.

An intuitive consultant and coach, she is also an author, speaker, and writer of many downloadable audio self-hypnosis series for adults and children. Rochelle is known as a life changer who makes sense out of trauma, including reframing relationships with others and the self. She can contribute expert counsel, intuitive insight, recovery action plans, routines and resolutions, case studies, and other information to support or enhance your article.

Rochelle is accredited with an M.A. in Spiritual Psychology and is a Certified Clinical Hypnotherapist, with additional certifications including PTSD. She is renowned for her depth of understanding on the spiritual dimensions of human nature and resolving emotional and habitual hurdles by working through root issues.

Rochelle has also served as an advisor and coach for a variety of film directors, producers, lawyers, doctors, and other public figures and professionals. She is a regularly invited guest speaker and workshop leader, including addressing thousands at St. Marks Cathedral on Capital Hill in Seattle. In addition, she has published journals and will release a much-anticipated book on weight loss in 2017.

Rochelle combines the practice of Hypnosis with Spiritual Psychology. **She specializes in abandonment and depression issues.** Besides her personal experiences, which allow her to deeply understand life's challenges, she has extensive training in the following areas: Gestalt, Carl Rogers's Person Centered Therapy, Piero Ferrucci Imagery Work, Inner Child Work and Guided Spiritual Journey work. She is a firm believer in William Glaser's Reality Therapy and Choice Theory.

Rochelle believes that we all have the answers deep within our selves. Uncovering underlying issues allows one to heal and move forward in life. Combining the practice of Spiritual Psychology and Hypnosis produces magical results. The subconscious mind is instructed to see the reality of the situation from the pure self-perspective, which allows misunderstandings and judgments to finally be forgiven for the very last time.

Early Praise for 7 Paths to Healing Your Relationship

"I love the idea of Rochelle's book and think there is tremendous value in understanding that your past relationships have everything to do with your current relationships."

> **Lisa J. Ling,** American journalist, television presenter and author, currently the host of *This is Life with Lisa Ling* on CNN

"Emotionally personal, immediately helpful, deep and beautiful. This book is a page-turner, a treasure box full of tools to help the soul. Rochelle's work is inspirational and helps others to reach within, and find the courage they need to take the next step."
> **Jonas Elrod** Writer/Director/Sherpa, acclaimed spiritual documentary *Wake Up* and *In Deep Shift.* OWN Network's Super Soul Sunday

"There is a lot of wisdom and solid material in this book for anyone struggling with a painful relationship."
> **Susan Forward,** Ph.D, LCSW, author of *Toxic Parents* and *Mothers Who Can't Love.*

"With her book, The Soul's Coach - 7 Paths to Healing Your Relationship," Rochelle L. Cook gives us a book that is truly helpful and needed. Relationships are the most important thing in our lives, but they are often neglected in favor of temporal goals. Whether you think you have a good relationship or not, or are looking for one, this book will give you very practical yet powerful tools to help you. I highly recommend Rochelle's important work."
> **Gary Renard,** best-selling author of *The Disappearance of the Universe* trilogy.

What Others are Saying

Rochelle is a guiding light for me.

I struggled for years with low self-esteem. It affected how I viewed family, job, world and myself. I tried reading books, articles and talking to friends and family but I was too afraid to see a therapist. My relationship with my parents was non-existent and I was so scared of what others thought about me. I was defensive with my siblings and boyfriend of 7 years. I was lost and had no idea who I was or where I was going. I was angry, sad, confused and lonely all the time, while outsiders thought I was amazing, fun, adventurous and smart.

About two months ago, I had enough and I knew that if I didn't fix myself, I would never move forward. I found Rochelle online and had a 15-minute phone call with her. She asked me why I was looking for help and I told her that no matter where I went or what I did, there was always a level that I couldn't get passed. I would reach a point (either at work or with love) and no matter what I did to try to get passed it, I couldn't jump because I was so scared to fail. She listened and she spoke and quickly honed in on how my childhood affected my present day. After those 15 minutes, it made me realize that I made the first step to healing myself and she made me feel like everything is going to be ok. That was the first time I felt like it would be.

After that, I went in for sessions with her. She asked me questions about my childhood. I couldn't stop crying. I felt my layers and negative thoughts peeling back slowly. She gave me exercises to do at home that gave me the opportunity to see who I am and how I saw myself. It hasn't been easy but I've been able to see how my self love and acceptance of my whole self, both good and bad.

My relationship with my parents has significantly improved and I'm able to handle problems more effectively without allowing others to sway me. My boyfriend, now recently fiancé, recently told me that he's seen how much I've grown and how much happier I am and I actually believe him now. I'm able to confront the negative thoughts that I was too scared or embarrassed to share with others, without self-judgment or hate. With Rochelle's help and guidance, I'm able to have compassion, love and respect for others, something I never would've been able to do without her commitment to my growth and well-being.

If you're considering getting help, I hope that you decide to allow her to help you.

Rochelle, you are a gift to my life and I am so incredibly grateful to you. Thank you.

R.C. Santa Monica, California, USA

Rochelle's work is a great guide for any executive looking for greater fulfillment and purpose and balance.

Television Executive, California, USA

Rochelle is excellent at what she does and I found her knowledge, her understanding and love for what she does to be so powerful. She really can get in deep and shift life patterns that hold you back. I know in my own life I have repeat the same painful patterns over and over again not anymore because of the wisdom and breakthrough work of Rochelle, thank you!

Lorna P. Naas, Republic of Ireland

I first met Rochelle a few years ago. I had never tried hypnotherapy before, but went in for my first session open to the experience and with a true commitment to the changes I needed to make in my life.

Rochelle was incredible. I remember the feeling after my first session: it was like I had taken a strong calming pill. I was so relaxed and light, it was kind of weird, but it felt great.

I worked weekly with Rochelle for about a month or two, and the blockages that I was experiencing for a long time were dismantled. It was that fast.

Overall, hypnotherapy is highly effective (at least it was for me) in changing even the most rooted habits and blockages in your mind/body. Of course, I give Rochelle all the credit on this -- she really knows what she's doing.

I wish I could see Rochelle every week of my life! Thanks so much Rochelle!

Michele G. Los Angeles, California, USA

I came to see Rochelle a few months ago; I have been suffering from a relationship breakup. Before I went to see her I spent my days extremely upset and unable to function. All I wanted to do was to get over the person who no longer wanted to be in my life. After the first session I noticed a difference, I did not feel so upset. A few sessions later I was over my heartbreak! Now I realize that I am better off without this person! We did the sessions all over Skype. Rochelle records all of the sessions so you can replay them. Thank you Rochelle for helping me. I feel so much better. If anyone is in pain I highly recommend seeing Rochelle. She is truly a lifesaver!

Tammy L. Sacramento, California, USA

Rochelle has helped me over the past two years with a number of issues. I have a hard time trusting in people, especially when it comes to my inner fears- I instantly connected with her! She has helped me to overcome my anxiety and help me start to live the life I have always wanted. Thank you! I recommend her for anyone that is looking to help himself or herself no matter the issue.

R.P. Seattle, WA

Rochelle is brilliant. I had read about her incredible work and desperately wanted to see her, but did not have the funds. Rochelle heard a bit of my story and has opened her arms (and beautiful space) to me for free. Truly a testament to her selflessness and dedication to her craft.

For years I have been depressed- and despite many other methods (including therapy, medication) I have been unable to feel better. I have only had two sessions with Rochelle and I swear the cloud of confusion and despair that has been surrounding me for so long has been lifted. The troubling elements in my life have become so much clearer and manageable. Rochelle imparts her wisdom and years of experience in a way that is simple to understand and easy to implement into your life. Rochelle has an energy about her that is completely one of a kind- rather, once in a lifetime! Just sitting with Rochelle brings me an air of tranquility. And each time I leave, I feel free of my troubles, empowered & (she says it best herself), THRIVING! She brings out the creative, happy and loving side of me that I often feel I am without. She has helped me to rediscover my sense of self, and helps me to see the beauty in me!

In this town, it is impossible to find someone so sincere, warm and passionate. She is in this business for the business of others. She just gets it. Although I've tried to portray how incredible she is, it is difficult to find words to accurately describe Rochelle. She is such a rare extraordinary talent. I feel so lucky to have found her, and cannot wait for her to continue to further shift my perceptions to help me embody a clearer mindset.

I have endless love for this woman!!! I can never thank you enough, Rochelle for helping me in this difficult time.

G.P. *Silver Lake, Los Angeles, USA*

I'm writing this review because I know how overwhelming it can be to carry and be deeply affected by unresolved trauma. The overwhelming piece comes in by thinking it's not possible to heal the underlying pain. I'm blown away by all that's happened in the short time I've been seeing (healing through) Rochelle. I'm working through extreme childhood trauma that my subconscious mind has held on to.

I was thrilled to find The Thriving Mind and Rochelle as hypnosis has helped me in the past (with less challenging things); her spiritual psychology expertise sealed the deal for me. With that, I had no idea I'd experience the depths of what's unfolding.

My first session was to tell my story. I was able to talk about it with a fair amount of ease, as Rochelle is warm, open and very compassionate; you definitely know she understands the depth of what you've been through. I was sent home with a very calming hypnosis mp3 that helped me to feel peaceful; I've never felt peaceful after sharing my horrendous childhood!

My next session connected me with my inner child through hypnosis. I was guided in a way that felt safe and loving. It was a healing and reconnection session that truly blew me away. It was a beautiful, heartfelt and joyous reunion with my child self, as odd as that may sound. My subconscious mind was able to go back to another time in my life. It was a vivid experience that included a loving exchange between the younger me and my current self that was needed to start the healing process.

I'm reading, writing (purging), writing some more and enjoying this healing process. Did I say enjoying!!! I would never have anticipated that, NEVER.

Rochelle is an amazingly gifted healer. I was guided to her and am tremendously grateful for all that's coming through. I can't wait for my next session and all that is to come.

I hope my thoughts will be helpful to someone looking for healing... There's a reason Rochelle has so many wonderful reviews. You can't help but want to let others know how life changing her work is.
Valerie J. Los Angeles, California, USA

I found Rochelle on Yelp. I thought, why not give it a try. I have gone to counseling on and off for years. Rochelle was the first person to really put her whole heart and soul into helping her clients. She knows what she is doing. She has made a huge difference in my thinking and overcoming my childhood issues. She is quick to call back and respond to any issues I may be facing. If you really want your issues to be resolved, you can rely on the program she uses. She will give you 100% because she cares so much!
Kelly R. Torrance, California, USA

Rochelle is a great therapist. She is very intuitive and knows how to really help those who are struggling. So glad to know her!
D J. Los Angeles, California, USA

I've had two sessions with Rochelle so far. The first one was two hours and the second one was 1 hour. Rochelle is very approachable, very caring and is quick at finding the deeper rooted reasons that brought you to her office, provide a customized hypnosis session and still find time to get to know you!

She is really knowledgeable in different aspects of spirituality, psychology and the related. I would definitely recommend her for anyone who is looking for someone to trust and work on himself or herself at a deeper level! You can tell that she really wants you to heal and realize your own potential.

I'm really happy to have found her

Helene V. Los Angeles, California, USA

Rochelle is able to make you feel uplifted and at peace, no matter what might be bothering you when you see her. Rochelle is genuine and can make you feel like you have known her your whole life. I have never felt so refreshed after speaking to someone about myself. Thank you, Rochelle

Laura C. Newport Beach, California, USA

Rochelle is an inspiring and intelligent person. She has helped me so quickly with so many deep rooted issues that I feel like I have been stuck with for so long. I cannot thank her enough for helping me start a new journey. Her technique works, and it is a wonderful to be in her company.

I have never tried hypnotherapy before, but I am so grateful to have found Rochelle because I have realized that is she gives so much more. She is an incredible spiritual guide, filled with light and love. I look forward to continue working with her.

I. W. Venice, California, USA

Rochelle is truly a remarkable person and is the best at what she does. What makes Rochelle different than anyone else I've ever worked with is that she LOVES what she does and is simply passionate about helping people and it shows through in her work! I've spent years in and out of therapy with small improvements. I've seen Rochelle about 4-5 times now and the progress and growth I've seen so far greatly surpasses what I saw in years of work with other practioners!

There are hardly words to describe the beautiful work she does. Beyond individual work with her patients, Rochelle spends a lot of time giving back to the community at large, especially the LGBT community. Rochelle really specializes in helping people with self-acceptance and abandonment issues, which devastatingly, is common within the LGBT community. Rochelle and a colleague of hers put on large seminars throughout the country for LGBT persons that work on healing through meditation called "Yes, I Belong". I encourage any LGBT brothers and sisters who are looking for someone to work with to seek out Rochelle or the large seminars she hosts. She knows her stuff.

So much love and gratitude for Rochelle.

Cecilia M. Los Angeles, California, USA

Rochelle helped me to recognize some deep-rooted issues I didn't realize I had buried way down. After a number of sessions, I feel more free and at peace. I don't think there are many therapists like Rochelle out there - her methodology is different yet works. I recommend her if you are seeking answers, want more awareness for yourself and are open to change... and doing the (necessary) homework that helps you to really heal. Rochelle knows her stuff!!!

C. G. Venice, California, USA

I contacted Rochelle because I needed help in recovering from a phone psychic addiction. For the past five years I had been calling psychics to get readings on my love and relationships. At first it started out as a few readings a month for insight and fun, but then my boyfriend left me, and I spiraled out of control. I was in severe emotional pain and needed to hear that he was going to return. At my worst I was getting 8 readings a day and spent $3500 in one month. I wish it were only one month that I did that but it was several. As new challenges came up in my life with new men and work dramas I found I couldn't stop calling. I knew I had a problem and did go to a local therapist in my first attempt at quitting. Everything we talked about sounded really good at the moment, but I was so sick I would call my psychics on the drive home from therapy. I had heard of people losing weight and quitting smoking with hypnotherapy so I thought if I could be hypnotized maybe I could break the habit. That's when I did some research and found then contacted Rochelle. On the first session she asked me several questions to get to the root of the issue. It did take a while and we ended up going a little over the time. At the end of that session she hypnotized me and I met my inner child. I wasn't completely cured at that moment but so much was revealed as to why I was calling and needing so much assurance all the time. Just having the answer to why I was calling gave an immediate shift on the way to healing. I have met with her a total of five times over the course of three months. Each time we talk about my current issues and she gives me hypnotherapy, which shifts my thinking to healthy thinking patterns. That scared inner gut feeling that I used to get all the time is gone now and I haven't called the network since starting therapy with Rochelle. I wholeheartedly recommend Rochelle to anyone battling any issues. She gets to the root not just the surface and you will feel the difference.

Sara A. Lancaster, California, USA

Rochelle is definitely passionate about healing others. I felt a connection with her from the moment I met her. She always makes room in her busy schedule for me, even on days when she's supposed to be off. I'm so fortunate to have her in my life!

Rica K. Mission Hills, California, USA

What an amazing experience! Rochelle is heaven sent. I had a friend that highly recommended her and never trying hypnosis before, I decided to give it a go. And I was glad I did. Rochelle is very knowledgeable and gifted. I recently went to Rochelle a few times and have started seen a transformation in myself. She makes you feel very comfortable and open. I am definitely going back and I recommend anyone who has ever given it a thought to try. And if you're a skeptic, a session will sure change your mind. Here is to health, wealth, and happiness!

Lucy L. San Diego, California, USA

When I met Rochelle I instantly realized that why I thought was coming in wasn't why I needed her. In our first session I was able to open up and have an instant breakthrough on a far deeper matter - issues around my Mother that I'd been carrying around for my entire 34-year existence. In her presence, in her understanding, I felt safe and could trust her. With Rochelle's help, her guidance, her hypnotherapy and specific homework instructions, I went from feeling total resentment and resistance towards my Mother to feeling compassion, love and recognition that my Mother is a part of me, and one that I highly value. How many sessions did this take? Five. Five incredible sessions that released a lifetime of pain and suffering. I'm a different person now and since I still have quite a few sessions left, we're now delving into another gross monster: limiting beliefs. I'm excited to do this work, to get more clearing, to make room for the self-actualized woman that I am becoming. I'm grateful for Rochelle and her transformative work.

Ada D. Los Angeles County, California, USA

Rochelle is SOOO GOOD @ what she does. I feel safe with her & confident that when hypnotized I can let go because I really trust her & know I'm in good hands. I always feel uplifted when leaving her office. She's extremely intuitive, gets to the heart of the matter, &

hypnotizes on whatever is needed most. I also like the zen, private, protective, good energy feel of her office. So glad I found her! :)

Mary M. Venice, California, USA

Purchased a session with her and have been going back weekly to her ever since. I was unfamiliar with hypnosis, but intrigued to learn and try to heal things that I felt needed to be addressed from my past. I am learning how powerful our subconscious really is. We so often forget the power of our minds since we usually are not aware of this subconscious level. I have been to therapy in the past, but nothing like this. I believe Rochelle is able to help me more than any other person I have found. She is effective. I tell her my life story, what bothers me, what I struggle with, and we spend our sessions repairing and envisioning the life that I want and actually have (if I let go of all the hurt, pain, and fears I have carried for so many years). I thank Rochelle for her insight, her ability to say exactly what I need to hear. My mind is humbled by her words. After each session I feel so happy. I have been raving about her since I met her. I HIGHLY recommend trying this out. She has a gift, and I am lucky I found her. My life seems to be happier already. Thank you!

Elina A. Los Angeles, California, USA

Rochelle is an amazing human being. She knows people just by spending a bit of time with them. Her eyes say it all, comforting, smart, warm loving person.

I would recommend her with anything she is doing because she gives it her all and she does everything so well

Margo C. Seattle, WA., USA

I had emotional damage that I couldn't get over, which led me to Rochelle about a month ago. I call her my therapist and coach because she's so much more than a hypnotist. I listen to her recording every other day and had substantial improvement. I went back two weeks later to talk about my progress and do another recording. I've referred her to my friends and family. I like her integrative approach. She's very real, intuitive and empathetic.

C.C Venice, California, USA

After getting nowhere with therapy for years, I found Rochelle. Her work has had a profound effect on my life in just weeks in a way therapy does not. She gets to the root of issues and helps clean them up immediately. You leave her office feeling safe every single time.

I highly recommend this to anyone who has issues with anxiety, relationships, and grief.

Mo. K Los Angles, California, USA

I've been seeing Rochelle for a little over a month now and the changes I have seen in my life are incredible. I have struggled for years with anxiety and specifically anxiety/fear surrounding my relationships. We are working together to combat and eliminate some of my deep-rooted fears and self esteem issues. I am so excited about the changes I have seen thus far and looking forward to what's to come with our continued work together. I have spent years with therapists trying to achieve what Rochelle has done for me in just one month. She is attentive, and available and most importantly, I feel she is truly invested in helping me on my journey to a healthier, happier life!

Lulu D. Playa del Rey, California, USA

Rochelle has practically saved my life! I have suffered from abandonment issues forever. Recently I lost my relationship. It seems like every time this happens to me I feel as though my world is ending. I would rate my reaction to loss as severe.

The first time I went to see Rochelle she helped me in just one visit. I have seen her a few times now and I cannot believe the difference. I'm not sure what she does but I can tell you she's magical. She is far more then the typical hypnotherapist. She does hypnosis and talks to you but something I cannot pin point also happens. Rochelle is a true healer.

Thank you Rochelle from the bottom of my heart. I do feel safe now and the nightmare I have faced throughout my entire life is over. You will never know how grateful I am. Thank you!

Cindy L. Marina del Rey, USA

I have had the extreme good fortune of encountering Rochelle in my life during the past couple of months. I did not know Rochelle before I decided to go to her for hypnotherapy. I randomly saw an ad for her hypnotherapy services. She had great reviews on yelp so I decided to give her a try. I have been plagued by panic, fear and anxiety for just about as long as I can remember and I just wanted to know what it would feel like to be "peaceful" and "normal" like other people must feel that don't have these issues. I'm in my mid 40's so I've been dealing with this for a very, very long time. The journey and literal life transformation that occurred as a result of working with Rochelle is nothing short of miraculous. Seriously. Shortly after I started seeing her my symptoms basically vanished. She enabled me to get past several traumatic events that had left these life lasting very, very negative emotions. She used a couple types of hypnotherapy including past life regression. Several years ago I saw a psychiatrist (nice but just talk, talk, talk - nothing resolved) and a psychologist/hypnotherapist (nice, still nothing resolved) and various anti-anxiety medications prescribed by doctors over the years to combat my feelings. If I had known that I could have resolved them by going to Rochelle, I would have done these years ago. I am thankful that I have been able to go through this journey with her. She is extremely knowledgeable, honest, straightforward, kind, compassionate and super easy to talk to - she made me feel immediately comfortable and there is an extremely healing and spiritual nature about her work. Rochelle is the real deal and I am truly thankful that she has been part of my healing journey towards a feeling of real peacefulness. If you can relate to this on any level, run to her, don't walk.....................for me, this has been one of the single most profound and healthy choices I have ever made for my mind, body and soul - in my entire life. If you are serious about making a life transforming change then go see Rochelle.

A. L. Hermosa Beach, California, USA

Afterword

Dedicated to my mother Lee.

Desiderata
by Max Ehrman

Go placidly amid the noise and the haste,

and remember what peace there may be in silence.

As far as possible, without surrender,

be on good terms with all persons.

Speak your truth quietly and clearly;

and listen to others,

even to the dull and the ignorant;

they too have their story.

Avoid loud and aggressive persons;

they are vexatious to the spirit.

If you compare yourself with others,

you may become vain or bitter,

for always there will be greater and lesser persons than yourself.

Enjoy your achievements as well as your plans.

Keep interested in your own career, however humble;

it is a real possession in the changing fortunes of time.

Exercise caution in your business affairs,

for the world is full of trickery.

But let this not blind you to what virtue there is;

many persons strive for high ideals,

and everywhere life is full of heroism.

Be yourself. Especially do not feign affection.

Neither be cynical about love,

for in the face of all aridity and disenchantment,

it is as perennial as the grass.

Take kindly the counsel of the years,

gracefully surrendering the things of youth.

Nurture strength of spirit to shield you in sudden misfortune.

But do not distress yourself with dark imaginings.

Many fears are born of fatigue and loneliness.

Beyond a wholesome discipline,

be gentle with yourself.

You are a child of the universe

no less than the trees and the stars;

you have a right to be here.

And whether or not it is clear to you,

no doubt the universe is unfolding as it should.

Therefore be at peace with God,

whatever you conceive Him to be.

And whatever your labors and aspirations,

in the noisy confusion of life,

keep peace in your soul.

With all its sham, drudgery, and broken dreams,

it is still a beautiful world.

Be cheerful. Strive to be happy.

N.B. American writer <u>Max Ehrmann</u> (1872–1945) a poet and lawyer wrote the prose poem "Desiderata" in 1927. After being inspired by a diary entry he made about desire (*Desiderata* is desire in Latin). In 1956, the Reverend Frederick Kates, <u>rector</u>of <u>Saint Paul's Church</u> in <u>Baltimore, Maryland</u>, included *Desiderata* in a compilation of devotional materials for his congregation. The compilation included the church's foundation date: "Old Saint Paul's Church, Baltimore <u>AD</u> 1692". Consequently, the date of the text's authorship was (and still is) widely mistaken as 1692, the year of the church's foundation.

Footprints in the Sand
by Mary Stevenson

One night I dreamed a dream.

As I was walking along the beach with my Lord.

Across the dark sky flashed scenes from my life.

For each scene, I noticed two sets of footprints in the sand,

One belonging to me and one to my Lord.

After the last scene of my life flashed before me,

I looked back at the footprints in the sand.

I noticed that at many times along the path of my life,

especially at the very lowest and saddest times,

there was only one set of footprints.

This really troubled me, so I asked the Lord about it.

"Lord, you said once I decided to follow you,

You'd walk with me all the way.

But I noticed that during the saddest and most troublesome times of my life,

there was only one set of footprints.

I don't understand why, when I needed You the most, You would leave me."